Phoenix in a Jade Bowl

Growing Up In Korea

Bonnie Bongwan Cho Oh

This book is dedicated to my
Parents,
Cho Pyong-chae and Koo Yon-soo,
who had to start over many times, and yet,
managed to send all seven children to college and
send six of them to study abroad.

ACKNOWLEDGMENT

I gratefully acknowledge the members of the Creative Writing Workshop of Northwestern University's Life-Long Learning Institute (OLLI) for their encouragement and constructive criticism. Special gratitude is due to Ann Fay for her reassuring comments, suggestions for revisions and referring me to an experienced editor, Gerard Higgins (Fitz).

Fitz was the first to suggest that I finish this project before I take on the challenge of revising a much longer manuscript on a historical figure. I am appreciative of his patience and detailed attention in picking out my quirks as a non-native English speaker. He corrected when necessary but preserved text that represented Asian cultural uniqueness.

Last, but not least, I belatedly express my gratitude to my late husband, John Kie-chiang Oh, for his unswerving support when I was beginning my graduate studies as a newly married woman in the early 1960s. My children's encouragement sustained me throughout the project.

CONTENT

East Asia: Korea and Her Neighbors, a map   xi
A Map of Korea, 1896-1948   xii
Korean Peninsula with the
38th parallel and the Armistice line, 1953   xiii

INTRODUCTION   15
Earliest Memories   19
Brother and Me   29
You Promised . . .   37
Pyongyang   43
Solo Train Ride   51
Grandma's Big House   57
Eels and Antlers   63
Name Conversion   69
A Liberation Baby   79
Ghosts Walking   85
A Nationalist   91
Awakening   97

The Outbreak of the War   105
Youth Volunteer Corps   113
Life under the North Korean Occupation   121
One-Four (1.4) Retreat   129
A Refugee Life   139
A Stealthy Preparation   147
Butterfinger   155
EPIOLOGUE   161
GLOSSARY   165
GEOEGRAPHICAL NAMES   169

PHOTOS

The first birthday table   41
My Father (1909-1968) in
Judge's Robe circa (1942)   50
Jesa sang (ancestral worship ceremony table)   77
A Middle School class photo, 1948   103
A map of North Korean invasion   112
General Macarthur's X Corps
Inch'on landing, 15 September 1950   128
Refugees trekking through
the blizzard of January 1951   135
Captain Oh at Panmunjom, Spring 1953   162
50th anniversary party, 30 August 2009 163
On the grounds of the Blue House,
3 August 2012   164

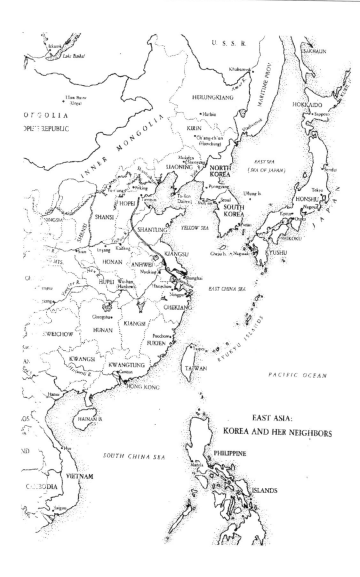

EAST ASIA:
KOREA AND HER NEIGHBORS

MAP OF KOREA, 1896–1948

The Korean peninsula with the 38th parallel and the Armistice line

INTRODUCTION

This is the story of my growing-up years in South Korea from the mid-1930s to early 1956, when I came to the United States to receive more substantial undergraduate education. South Korea was in the throes of reconstruction—both chaotic and uneven—after the end of the Koran War, which lasted three years and left a devastated country in ruins. Little learning went on even in the most prominent institution of higher education in Korea, Seoul National University. My desire to lay a firm intellectual foundation for my adult life during my undergraduate years overcame all possible negative consequences of leaving my parents and home for the first time in my life. Never did it occur to me at the time that I would not return to my native land to live but instead make a home in this country. I came to study for just a few years. I have now lived in United States for 57 years.

The title, "Phoenix in a Jade Bowl," is the literal translation of my given name Bongwan. American colleagues and friends know me as Bonnie Oh. But before Bonnie Oh, I was Bongwan Cho, and I still use the first letters of my natal name as my middle initials and use them as my email address. I changed Bongwan to Bonnie in order to make life simpler, for when I was at Barnard College in New York in the 1950s, I received many questions and complaints about my name. Some wanted to know if there was a special meaning and others thought that it was too difficult to pronounce.

In the beginning, I carefully explained every time some one asked me that my given name consisted of two Chinese characters—as most Korean names do. The first is "bong," which means, "phoenix," and the second, "wan," which means "a jade bowl." But it got to be too much of a hassle to explain each time I met a new girl in my class or the dorm. It also bothered me to hear that my name was too hard to articulate, and some of them started calling me by only the half of the name, "Bong," which made me feel that I was cut in half, like a woman in a magic show. I searched for a homonym for "Bong" and settled on Bonnie with the help of a group of my close friends and formalized it at the college's registrar's office. My friends thought it suited me well. I obviously acted unfilially to my father by changing the name he carefully chose, but I also knew that he was an educated, tolerant person and that he would at least acquiesce, if not approve, of my practical decision.

In Korea, and in other Asian countries for that matter, naming a child had long been an important responsibility for parents, especially in the case of a male infant. The Cho clan, my natal family, had generational names for hundreds of years and had been duly noted in genealogy books, and my ancestors used them dutifully. They had to take into account at least three factors. First, there is a generational name character that would apply to all male children born in the same cohort in the entire clan. For example, my husband gave a character "Tak," meaning "brilliant," to all four of our Oh grandsons. Second, there is the consideration of geomancy, "p'ung-su," (or feng sui in Chinese) to make sure if the character suited the child's destiny according to the rule of the universe. Finally, there is the character's suitability as an adult name.

For a baby girl, it was different. Until the end of the nineteenth century, a female infant would not often have a specific name. She was not important enough. She would simply be called, "the first," "second," or—heaven forbid—"third daughter" of xxx family. By the time I was born, however, things had changed.

When my generation of children was born, my father and his older brother decided that the letter assigned to our group was known to be unlucky according to geomancers' finding. My uncle, therefore, did not name his only son according to the tradition. That freed my dad from following the age-old practice, and he could do whatever he wished in naming his children. To my father, it mattered little that I, his first-born, was not a son. He took naming me seriously and gave me a name that is not a typical female name. It is possible that receiving pre-collegiate education at Paejae Boys' High School influenced him not to be obsessed with "boy preference" custom in Korea. His high school was the first institution of modern education for young men, established by American Presbyterian missionaries in 1884.

While in elementary school, I was often taunted because my name sounded like a boy's. When I asked my father why he had named me so, he explained his thinking.

"I wanted you to know and believe," he told me, "that even though you are a girl you don't have to feel limited to being a female. A typical girl's name can prejudice a child from an early age. I also wanted you to be a strong enough person to rise from the ashes like a phoenix (bong), a legendary bird, but at the same time, be grounded (wan) in a solid jade bowl."

"So, you wanted me to soar," I replied, "but not to roam wild and then come home to the nest?"

"Yes, you've got it, my daughter."

I am grounded all right, but soaring, I am not so sure.

CHAPTER 1:

EARLIEST MEMORIES

It was mid-morning of an early sunny winter day. I was watching Mom grooming herself sitting on a cushion at the *maru*, a center hall of a Korean traditional house. The north wall of the *maru* had semi-lucent glass panels and against it were a glass cabinet of fine china in the center, a *duiju* (rice chest) on the right and a *bandaji* (a storage chest) on the left. Compared with the one at Grandmother's house, it was a small *maru*, but it was neat and tidy. The floor was beautifully varnished and the sun was shining through the glass panel of sliding doors facing south. Mom was sitting in front of a medium sized three-panel make-up stand, which she used to take out from the room on the east of the *maru* after Dad left for work. My baby brother and I shared the room on its west side across from the one Mom and Dad used. Brother was sleeping after his breakfast; the maid was washing the morning dishes in the kitchen located to the front right of the *maru*. I loved such quiet mid-morning times with Mom.

My mother, Koo Yon-su (women kept their maiden names), was four years younger than my father, Cho Pyong-chae. She was a petite slender person with a good-looking, light skinned face. She was always neat. I never saw her in nightclothes or unruly hair. She dressed in the Korean-style outfit, of *chogori*, short jacket, and *chima*, full wrap-around skirt. Her black shiny hair was pulled back in a bun at the neck, secured with *binyo*, hairpin of gold, silver or jade, which she changed seasonally. She had a mannerism of a refined lady, proper and polite. She totally dedicated herself to taking care of my father and us. She prepared the food and took care of my father's work clothes, Western-style shirt and suit herself although she had an all-purpose helper. She was also a dedicated mother for my brother and me. She was a perfect model of *hyon-mo yang-ch'o,* a wise mother and a good wife. If my mother wished to be anything other than being a good mother and wife, we had no hint of it.

She was believed to have been the smartest of my grandparents' eight children, four sons and four daughters and graduated from Kyunggi Girls' High School, the most highly regarded school for young women. In addition to being a good student, despite her long-distance commuting from Inch'on, a harbor city on the west coast, to Seoul, she was a ping-pong player and was voted the best dressed all through her high school years. She wanted to continue her education, but there was no college for women at the time in Korea. Only way was to go abroad, and a few women who sought higher education went to Japan. But my grandparents would not hear of it. Rumors of loose morality among female students studying abroad were rampant in the late 1920s and early 1930s Korea. She reportedly fasted for three weeks to plead her case, but she could not persuade her father.

As I watched her groom herself, I would poke my index finger on the facial power and lip paste, put them on my face, and force myself in front of Mom to look in the mirror. I looked quite funny: I had partially powdered my face and put lipstick all over my cheeks.

"Yew, I don't look good like you, Mom." I pouted.

"It's because you don't know how to put cosmetics on, and you are too young to use them. Besides, you don't need them yet." Mom gently pulled me over hugged me and wiped the stuff from my face.

"There," she said, "Now, you look in and see."

"Oh yeah. Now I look like me."

"That's how you want to look. You don't need any make-ups for a long time." Mom patted me on my back and said.

"Now run along. I want to check on your brother after I bring this thing into the room."

"Yeh, yes, *Umma*. I'll go in with you when you check on the baby."

"Sure, that'll be fine." I waited until she came back out from her room. I held Mom's hand and went into the room where my brother was taking a morning nap.

Brother Tonsung was a handsome, smart, and gentle kid. He was two years younger than I, but in size and smarts, he had almost caught up with me. He and I played well together. We drew pictures, wrote *han'gul,* Korean alphabets, which was prohibited from use outside home under the Japanese colonial rule. I had already learned to read and write in Korean and taught my brother to scribble "*umma* (mom) and *appa* (papa or dad) in our own language. My dad insisted that I learn Korean before I entered elementary school, where only Japanese was taught.

Our little house was on Daok-dong, a short street at the center of the capital city of Korea, Seoul. It was close to the main commercial street of Chongno, where the country's largest department store of the time, Hwashin, was located and the daily night market along the Ch'onggye-ch'on River provided the atmosphere of never-ending daylight. It was also close to my grandparents' big house. Many an evening, my uncles, my mother's single younger brothers, would stop by and take me out to treat me to *jjajangmyon,* noodles with black bean sauce, my favorite. I would hop, skip and jump, holding an uncle's hand and looking at trinkets on venders' carts. I never asked for anything as Mom told me not to, but my uncles would buy me hairpins and other stuff if I looked at an item long enough. One evening, my uncle bought me a strangely shaped bird made of gold-color wires. I neither looked at it long nor did I ask him to buy it for me. When I looked at him quizzically, he said,

"This is shaped like a phoenix, also known as fire-bird. The first character of your name, 'Bong,' means just that. So I thought you might like to have it."

"What is so special about it?" I asked.

"It's a legendary bird, which is supposed to have died in flames and is reborn from the ashes."

"Why did my Dad name me with the character, 'phoenix,' Uncle? I don't like it because it sounds like a boy's name."

"I don't know. My guess is that your dad wanted you to be a strong person who can rise again and again even after life's failings."

"Uhm?" I didn't quite understand what my uncle told me, but I remembered his explanation about the first of the two characters of my given name. I had to leave it there that evening to ask my dad later for we reached my favorite black-bean noodle eatery.

My grandma also visited us often. I never knew her full name while growing up. Much later I found out that she did have a full name, Yi Yong-sun, which was rare in her generation. She was shorter and slightly fuller in figure than Mom. She always wore traditional attire, usually in light colors, white in the summer, lavender in the spring and gray in winter. She did not receive formal education because there was no school for girls when she was growing up, but she was good with numbers, quick in wits and superb in inter-personal relationship. She held the purse strings and managed a huge traditional-style house with more than twenty residents: her stern husband, her eighties mother-in-law, her three married sons with their families, and scores of household helpers. She was a matriarch in its true sense.

It appeared that my mother was her favorite daughter. She visited us more often than her other daughters' homes. Whenever she came, she brought lots of things, the stuff that grandpa and she did not have a chance to give to my mom at the time of my parents' marriage and the items that my parents could not afford. My grandma felt sorry for Mom who, I heard, was the only one of her four daughters to marry a man without much inherited wealth. Mom, however, did not feel that she was deprived because of my dad's career prospects in law with a coveted degree from Keijo Imperial University, later Seoul National University. Because of my dad's superior education, his in-laws treated him deferentially although he was one of the youngest male members of the extended family.

Mother constantly reminded Grandma that my dad emphasized living within our means and that he did not approve of Grandma bringing expensive goods to us. The first time I observed my parents arguing was about just that. Grandma had brought us an embroidered multipanel silk *byongp'ung*, a paneled screen, which was set up at the drafty corner of my parents' room. As Dad walked in in the evening, he immediately noticed it.

"Where did this come from?" Dad asked Mom pointing at the thing.

"My mom got it for me because I am just a month away from delivering a baby and she thought that draft in the room was not good for an expectant mother. The *byongp'ung* will shield the cold air." Mom answered.

"As I told you many times, you have to manage with the salary I am bringing to you. You had known when we got married that I was not a rich man and I had no inheritance for I used it to pay for my modern education at Paejae high school and Keijo Imperial University." I was stunned to hear that my father's usual gentle voice changed to firm, louder declaration.

My father was not tall, but he more than made it up with handsome face and dignified air. You might say he had charisma. To me, he was never overly serious but always gentle and nice, which was contrary to most fathers were supposed to be at that time in Korea. In the 1930s Korean thinking, fathers were to be strict and not show emotions to children.

"Please take it back right away after the dinner tonight. I don't want to have it sitting around in my house." Mom was already crying.

"You don't have to be so straight like a bamboo stick. My parents have so many of those things that they won't miss it even if they gave me one."

"No, I don't want anything that I cannot afford. Return it right away and come back immediately. And I don't want you crying there."

The dinner that night was quiet. I did not say anything either for fear of offending my parents. Mom hardly ate anything. After the dinner, Mom changed her clothes, asked me to get ready to go with her, and gave the maid instructions for my brother. A rickshaw was waiting for us outside our gate. Dad followed us with the panel and loaded it behind the passenger seat. Dad padded me on the back and said,

"My big girl, take care of Mom, Ok?" He sounded softer than before. But I was still scared because I had not seen Dad so upset.

"Yeh (yes), *tanyo oketsumnida*, we will be back, *ahboji*, father." I was careful to use more reverential, "ahboji," rather than "appa" in responding and bowing deeply to Dad. He turned to the paddy cab operator and told him,

"*Yoboshiu, jal butak haeyo*, hope you be good to them. As you can see my wife is expecting soon. Please avoid bumps on the road." He turned around and went inside the house.

Mother and I got on the rickshaw and rested my head on Mom's lap. We let our bodies be rocked to and fro by its movement. I cautiously looked at Mom. She was still sniffling.

"Mom, don't you think Dad is thoughtful. Even when he is troubled, he was concerned and called a paddy cab for us. Isn't he nice?"

"Only if he wasn't so obstinate . . ."

"But he loves you, Mom, and me too."

"I guess you are right." Mom turned to me, smiled and held my hand tight. Her eyes were red and swollen.

It didn't take long to reach my grandparents' house. The paddy cab operator gently put his handle down, stepped over it, approached the huge varnished two panel wood gates and called out,

"*Yoboseyo*, anybody home?" With a loud squeak, the gate opened and a man, a gatekeeper, stuck his head out through the opening.

"*Nuguseyo*, who is it?" He saw a rickshaw, opened the gates wider, came running to it and lifted its flap, and looked up at Mom and me.

"*Assi*, madam, what are you doing at this time of the night? Please come in." But Mom shook her head and told the man to take down the panel and give it to Grandma. She said that it was late and she needed to return home and that she would call Grandma the next morning to explain the situation. She did not even get off the vehicle and we headed back home immediately.

The next morning, Dad approached Mom, put her two hands into his and said,

"Are you still angry?" Mom rolled her eyes and said,

"At least you know you hurt me. Don't be such a straight arrow, OK?"

"As long as you do not go against my basic principles," was Dad's answer, "you know I give you my entire salary and leave you alone running the household in general, right?"

"All right, whatever you say. You are going to be late, get going." Mom gently shoved Dad out the door as she was smiling.

"See you later. Be good to Mom, my girl."

"Yes, of course, *Appa*." I responded.

He was out the courtyard and the main gate of the house.

Thereafter I became aware that my parents argued once in a while but their quarrels were never boisterous and did not last long. It was usually my father, who took the initiative to reconcile regardless of the causes of disagreement. I became aware later that this usually did not happen in most Korean households of the time. Men were always right and women had to follow their spouses' dictates. Husbands were supposed to be *soch'on*, small heaven.

All in all, my earliest memories were tranquil, peaceful, and happy. Although my parents seldom verbalized the word, *sarang*, love, I knew that my parents loved each other a lot and my brother and me as well. Little did I know that such serenity would come to a screeching halt toward the end of that year. I was four but five by Korean counting.

CHAPTER 2:

BROTHER AND ME

In the fall of 1938, my mom was expecting her third child. A few weeks before the expected date of the baby's arrival, she sent Brother Tonsung and me to our grandparents' house so that she could rest. Early one evening after supper, Grandmother came in a rickshaw to get us. Carrying small satchels holding our clothing and other personal belongings, we followed her out the door into the hand-driven vehicle. Mom and Dad came out the main gate and saw us off. They told us to behave and to be obedient to Great Grandma, Grandpa, Uncles, Aunts, and Cousins in the house. They told me that since my brother and I would be the youngest in the entire household, we needed to be respectful to all and that I, as the older sister, was responsible for my brother. I responded cheerfully then bowed my head to bid them farewell. We were supposed to be gone for about a month.

I was already inside the vehicle, when I heard Brother Tonsung throwing up a tantrum and refusing to get on. It was unusual for him to put up a fuss. He was normally a placid child. I heard Mom explaining to Grandma that he did not understand what was going on despite her efforts to prepare him for the trip. Dad picked Tonsung up and put him inside the cab, seated him next to me, told him sternly to be quiet, and helped Grandma to get on. Tonsung continued to cry even after we started to move. I pulled him close to me, patted him on the back, and hummed a lullaby. In a little while, he fell asleep on my lap, still sniffling. Grandma gently propped up his head on her lap, saying he was too heavy for me. I looked at Grandmother. She looked at me. We both smiled at the same time. I looked outside through a small vinyl window in one of the rickshaw's side flaps. The flap was secured with a couple of ties on the both sides. It did not close tightly and whiffs of chilly fall wind swooshed in as the rickshaw rolled on.

Soon we came to the front of the big, two-paneled wooden gates. Even in the dim streetlight, the gates' shiny varnish glistened. Hanging high in the center was a wrought-iron light fixture with an opaque globe bulb, which cast a dim light on the doorway. The rickshaw man gently lowered his vehicle to the ground, stepped over the handle bar, and walked to the front gate.

"*Yobosiu*," he hollered, "*kun manim oshutsiu*. Look here, senior lady is home. Please open the door and hurry. There are two little children and it's chilly."

"*Yeh*, I will be right there," a man's voice replied from within. With a loud squeak, the both sides of the gate opened. A middle-aged man with wrinkled face in rough cotton *chogori* and *paji* (pants) came out. I knew that he was the chief servant, a kind of a butler, and also the gatekeeper of the house. He and his wife lived with a son, Chang-kyu, in the outer quarter of the house, close to the main gate. His wife worked in the kitchen as one of the cooks. I knew neither his, nor his wife's, names. We called them Chang-kyu's Mom and Dad. We seldom called adults by their names. It was considered disrespectful. He quickly came over to the vehicle, lifted the side flap, looked inside and made a deep bow.

"Senior lady," he said respectfully, "you have arrived. We've been waiting for you."

"The boy cried and it took a while to calm him down," Grandma explained. Please bring him in and do so carefully," she bid him. "He's sleeping."

"Yeh-h-h . . ." Chang-kyu's pa answered.

The main gate opened up into an entrance way dimly lit with a hanging lamp. We entered the gate in the center. Beyond it was a beautifully landscaped courtyard with a round island that appeared to me like a small jungle of trees, bushes, and tiny waterfalls.

Our grandparents' home was a huge traditional Korean house with three separate complexes. There were the *sarang ch'ae*, or outer area, the *anch'ae*, the largest inner compound, and the *duit ch'ae*, the rear servant quarters.

Grandma led us to the *anbang*, the inner room to the left of the great center hall. The largest room in the house, the *anbang* belonged to her as matriarch. She opened the big, double-sided sliding doors, their latticework covered with translucent paper. I liked rice-paper sliding doors. They were weightless, easy to open, and let the light through without showing the interior. The room was large with a shiny yellow-colored, *ondol* floor, at the center of which was a red and blue embroidered *bolyo*, or thick mat. On the opposite side to the main doors was another set of smaller rice-papered doors, which led to the backyard, kitchen and rear complex. The left wall had a four sliding panels decorated with brush-paintings of flowers, landscapes, and calligraphy. Behind the door was the *darak,* or a pantry, a cavernous storage area where Grandma stored linens as well as dried goods, including candies and cookies. The *darak* was off-limits to everyone except Grandma, but she allowed me to go in and get snacks from the lower shelves. I had to keep this privilege secret from my cousins.

Facing the *darak* on the opposite wall were three big black lacquer wardrobes with inlaid designs in mother-of-pearl. These designs were a phoenix motif for Grandma's and a dragon for Grandpa's. The wardrobe closest to the main doors was Grandpa's, which had a long mirror on the left side and two paneled doors on the right. They opened up on to the hanging area of Grandpa's Western-style suits. Below them were drawers for other clothes, which could be folded flat. Grandma's center bureau had an eye-level shelf, where she kept her portable make-up stand also made of black lacquer with inlaid mother-of-pearl designs. All these were much bigger and more luxurious than those I saw at my house.

Since Grandpa came to the room only to get dressed in the morning, Tonsung and I slept in the room with Grandmother. I slept on a thick satin mat next to Grandma, and Tonsung slept next to me. This was considered such a privilege that my cousins were jealous of us.

Grandpa had a compound of his own, the *sarang ch'ae*, or man's quarter, which was located on the west side of the house and consisted of a hall to receive guests, a study, a bedroom, and an errand-boy's room. My grandfather, Koo Ch'ang-jo, was a self-made man of considerable wealth. By the time I knew him, he reportedly owned properties in two southern provinces and business establishments in Seoul and Inch'on. Grandpa had received no formal education but was a man with sharp wits and great intelligence. By the standard of the time, he was of medium height. Grandpa had a handsome face, with bright eyes, a white mustache, and thick, white hair. He always dressed in dark, meticulously tailored, Western-style suits. He had a regal bearing and serious look, which he maintained to everyone except his wife and his mother. Then in her eighties, my great-grandmother lived across the hall from the *anbang*. Grandpa was gentle to his mother and visited her every morning to pay his respects and inquire about her health. I remember being awed by his looks and presence, and impressed with his dedication to his mother. When Grandpa was around, everyone in the house tiptoed around. But I was not afraid of him because he held my brother and me in his arms and gave us pecks on our cheeks. Perhaps this was because we were just visiting.

Every one in the big house was nice to us. They obviously felt sorry that we were separated from our parents, even for a little while. The oldest uncle had three sons, Hah-soh, Ik-soh, and Jong-soh, and lived in a compound on the east side of the house a few steps down from the main *maru*. The second uncle with his wife and a daughter my age, Hye-soh, lived in a room, a couple of steps down from the oldest uncle's living area, facing the *maru*. On the same level as the second uncle on the west side of the courtyard lived a newly married third uncle with a baby son. His wife was a Japanese, who wore Western-style clothes. Her short, curly hair with permanent, looked quite different from that of the wives of the first and second uncles'.

The next morning, Brother Tonsung was fine and did not fuss. I was relieved. He seemed to have gotten over his tantrum of the night before. His happy disposition came back. He ate and played well with me, following me around wherever I went. We had many places to explore and a much wider area to play in than at our own house. I always liked visiting my grandmother, for she let me do a lot of things Mom did not allow. Grandma also looked after us with special care and shielded us from older male cousins. Still I did miss my parents and our home but I could not say it openly for fear of reminding my brother of Mom and Dad. Whenever we had quiet moments, he would begin to whine.

"*Noona* (big sister)," he asked, "when are we going home?"

"When Mom has the new baby."

"When is that going to be?"

"In a few days."

"How many more days are a few days?" Tonsung retorted. "You said the same thing for many days now."

Conversations like this occurred over and over in the course of a week. About ten days after we came to Grandparents' house, we heard the news that mom had safely delivered a baby girl and that my parents named her Bongsoon.

Tonsung jumped up and down.

"Now we can go home, right, sister?" he said loudly.

"No, not yet, not until Mom is stronger. A new baby is a lot of work. She has to rest for a while before we can go home." I was repeating what Grandma had told me. Even before I finished talking, my brother began wailing.

"I want to go home," he cried. "I want my mommy. I want my mommy." Although all my uncles and aunts tried to calm him down, Tonsung cried nonstop until he became so exhausted that he could not continue. Grandma and I hoped that he would be fine the next day. But his fussing continued, his appetite and energy dropped. Instead of actively playing, he would just sit or lie down, constantly singsonging, "I want my mommy. I want my mommy . . ."

Finally on the seventh day after the birth of my sister, Bongsoon, Grandma brought my brother and me home. For the first few days after we returned home, my brother was happy, ate and played well. But whenever he saw Mom with the new baby, he tried to yank her away and cling to Mom. My parents tried to reason with him, be stern with him, and bribe him. But nothing worked. When he realized that the baby was here to stay and he could not have Mom to himself any more, he fussed and cried. He began to look listless and pale.

CHAPTER 3:

YOU PROMISED . . .

The autumn was deepening. The chilly wind was blowing the fallen leaves, which sometimes rose into whirlwinds. The flowers in our small courtyard had mostly faded. Even the brilliant red and yellow chrysanthemums had faded in color. I would sit all by myself on the sunny steps leading to the yard wishing that my brother would come out to play. I would go into his bedroom to ask him, but when I saw him, I did not dare. He did not look like the boy I had known. Some days he was hot and agitated. Other days he was pale and quiet. Doctors and nurses came and went. They gave him shots and prescribed medicines.

Mom turned over the care of her newborn baby, Bongsoon, to a wet-nurse and dedicated her whole time to caring for Tonsung. But his condition did not improve and he had to stay in bed most of the time. I would go in and out just in case he felt like playing with me. When he saw me, he would smile and put his hand out to hold mine, but he could not get up. And I did not nag him.

Dad even took a few days off from work to stay with Tonsung, which was very rare. Grandma came and stayed in my room. Aunts and uncles visited us. I used to like to have them come because they brought good things to eat—roasted chestnuts, chestnut-filled bun cakes, candies, and even chocolates—but now their visits did not please me. They stayed only a short while and left looking glum. I received little cheerful response even when I tried to entertain them. I was beginning to feel sad myself. Instead of playing with toys I had always played with my brother, now I started to go into corners and sit quietly. Sometimes, I cried even while playing, walking around, eating, and going to bed. After a while, Mom asked Grandma to take me to her house.

Unlike other times that I had enjoyed going to Grandma's big house, I did not want to go. Mom said it would only be a few days until Tonsung got better. I made her promise that she would take a good care of my brother. She pledged to me with her hands folded together in prayer style. Before I left, I went to see Tonsung. He was half asleep. I gently shook his shoulder. He opened his eyes. His eyes were colorless. He forced a smile. Mom told me to leave him alone, but I put my mouth close to his ear.

"Get better, Tonsung," I whispered, "I will be back soon. Then, we'll play again as we used to."

"I promise, *noona*, older sister, I promise," Tonsung whispered, nodding to me.

Mom pulled me up to tell me that Grandma was waiting for me. Her big, splendid house no longer looked good to me. I did not feel happy, as I had been when I went there before with my brother. All the attention and love Grandma and other relatives showered on me did not improve my mood. Even the mischievous cousins were nice to me, but I did not care. I did not eat and sleep well. I tagged along behind Grandma everywhere she went in the house and nagged her to take me home to see my brother. Grandma could not cheer me up with all her goodies to eat and even some shiny coins that she put into my pockets.

On the third day in the afternoon, Grandma brought me home. I rushed into the yard to tell Mom that I was home. The wet-nurse, who was carrying my baby sister on her back, stopped and hushed me.

"Be quiet, your brother is not well."

"But he promised. He promised me he would get better. Besides, he's had his first birthday, and he's not supposed to get sick after his first birthday." I vaguely remembered his big first birthday party and recalled hearing that if the babies survived their first birthdays, they were supposed to live long. *He had his first birthday and he will get better.* I reassured myself. I was starting up the steps from the yard to see him.

"No, no, you can't go in. Your mom told me to keep you with me."

"No-o-o, I want to see my brother!" I hollered.

"Bongwan, please stay with me." Grandma held me tight from my back.

That night, I slept with Grandma in the room across the *maru* from where my brother was. Mom and Dad were with him. I snuggled deep into grandma's bosom and sniffled myself to sleep. In a dream I saw my brother, waving goodbye to me. I tried to get up to respond to him, but no words came out and I could not reach him. When I opened my eyes and sat up I was still in bed next to Grandma. I laid back and tried to fall back to sleep. I looked toward the sliding door facing the courtyard. The day was breaking. I heard Mom and Dad crying out for my brother. I got up from the bed to go see Mom and Dad, but Grandma held me back, she held me tight and rocked me back to sleep.

The noises outside awakened me. I looked around and Grandmother was not there. The room was bright with sunlight filtering through the rice-paper-latticed door. I slid it open a crack and peaked outside. There was a small white box in the middle of the yard, and all kinds of people were standing around it. Mom was kneeling down with her head and hands touching the box and crying. Dad was standing behind her with his one hand on her shoulder and wiping his eyes with the other. Two of my uncles approached Mom, and gently tried to lift her, to move her from away the box. She resisted at first but soon gave in. She first stood up, then turned around and huddled against Dad. He put his arms around her. Several male relatives surrounded the box, pulled up the ropes that lay underneath it, lifted the box, and started moving toward the gate.

I sprang up, still in my nightclothes, and dashed out to the room across. Tonsung's bed was empty. I flung down to the courtyard barefoot and ran to the moving box.

"Tonsung-ah, you can't go. You promised, you promised you'd get well . . ."

A boy's traditional first birthday table

CHAPTER 4:

PYONGYANG

In the late spring of 1939, a half-year after my brother died, we moved to Pyongyang in South Pyong-an province. Pyongyang is located a little over 120 miles north from Seoul, which was considered far at the time but was easily accessible by rail. The Taedong River, the fifth longest river in Korea, runs through the city. It is a historic city and had long been called the Second or Western Capital during the Yi Dynasty (1392-1910). It is now the capital of North Korea.

We had to move there, for Dad passed the civil service examination in the law division and was appointed a judge of the District Court of Pyongyang. Shortly before our departure from Seoul, relatives gathered to congratulate Dad and celebrate this rare honor in the family. There was a restrictive quota for Koreans for such positions in the government, and Koreans were required to have higher scores for the test than Japanese candidates. I heard that it was almost as hard as "catching a star."

But Mom was not overjoyed. She had always lived close to her parents and had never left Seoul since graduating from high school. Moving away from her parents to live in a strange city with two little girls was the last thing she wanted, especially so soon after her son's death. I, on the other hand, was proud of my father and looked forward to living in a new house in a different city.

We settled in a brand-new, Western-style house built for government officials. Our house, the only one occupied by a Korean family, was the last of the three almost identical looking houses in a row at the foot of the Moran-bong, the dogwood peak, and on the bank of a shallow stream. On the other side of the stream was a wide, open field with dandelions in bloom in the spring, which appeared to me like a sheet of gold. Dad was busy at his new job, Mom was sick often, a nanny took care of my baby sister, and I was alone. The crystal clear stream with minnows that flowed next to our house provided me a wonderful playground.

That first summer, Mom got so sick that Grandma came and took her back to Seoul to get intensive medical treatment and some rest. She was gone just for the summer months, but to me it seemed like an eternity. I would be in the creek for hours chasing after minnows and picking dandelions on the other side of the creek to make a bouquet for my mom, just in case she returned when I got home. I would also walk up and down the street lined with trees and high walls and look in the direction of the big street that crossed our side road to see if Mom was coming home.

When the morning and evening air became chilly, Mom came home with Grandma. Mom was still not completely well and was resting most of the time, and Grandma told me that Mom was much better, but continued to need lots of quiet time, and that I should not bother her too much. It was fine with me, at least for now. I had both Mom and Grandma, neither of whom I had had all summer. I especially loved having Grandma around for she doted on me.

As the fall semester was about to begin, a male cousin, of whom my parents had been telling me, arrived at our house. His given name was Soon, a one-character name, unlike mine and most of other Koreans' multi-syllable ones. He was the only son of Dad's older brother living on a family estate outside the city of Kangnung, in Kangwon Province, my father's ancestral home on the Korean peninsula's east coast. Dad told me Cousin Soon would live with us to attend the middle school, for schools in the urban areas were better than in the countryside and he had reached the middle-school age, an important stage for his future success. He was enrolled in Yi-Jung boys' school. Yi-Jung meant "number two middle" and was for high-caliber Korean students while Il-jung, "number one middle," was exclusively reserved for sons of high-ranking Japanese officials in the Pyongyang area.

Cousin Soon's room was at the end of a long corridor from the rooms for my parents and for my sister and me. At first, I used to peek into the room and watch him seated at the far end of the room on a cushion with a low desk in front of him. I noticed that he studied all the time. I was much impressed and got the idea that I should study with him.

One day after supper, I mustered up the courage and poked my head in and asked.

"*Oppa* (older male sibling), may I come in?"

"Oh, it's you, Bongwan, You should be getting ready for bed soon. What brings you here?'

"I brought you some cookies and the *boricha*, roasted barley tea."

"Thank you, did auntie give you this for me?"

"Yes, she prepared, but I volunteered to bring them for you. I also want to ask you if I may bring my home-work here and study with you after supper. I won't bother you and will be quiet, promise."

He stood up, took the cookies and tea tray from me with one hand, and ruffled my hair with the other.

"Sure, of course. I like that. It's lonely being away from my parents, you know."

"It's lonely for you? You are almost grown up, and I thought grown-ups don't get lonely. Is this the first time to be separated from your parents?"

"Yes, I miss home, and I am not grown up. I am only in middle school." He replied.

"You look grown up to me." I commented looking up. He laughed and said,

"But now that you are going to come and keep me company while studying, I will be much less so."

"Thank you, *Oppa*."

From then on, I went with cookies and tea to Cousin Soon's room after dinner, sat across the desk from him and did my homework. As a first-grader, I did not have enough homework to fill the whole evening, but I stayed in my cousin's room until Mom called me to get ready for bed. I quietly did my homework, drew pictures and read. Much later in my life, I realized that mimicking my older cousin's study habits helped me.

A year after Cousin Soon came to live with us, I had another sister, Ugza, the third daughter for my parents. Mom was mortified that she had a third daughter. The thought of not having a son to carry on Dad's name bothered Mom although it did not seem to trouble Dad as much. The household became quite busy and full, which I liked. But it appeared that it was a lot to handle for my mother, who did not have a strong constitution. Dad's government salary was hardly sufficient to cover the cost of a family of seven, including a young babysitter. Also, often times, my aunt, Mom's oldest sister, visited from Ch'ung-ch'ong province, southwestern "rice bowl" area of the country, where Grandpa also had an extended property, and stayed months at a time. She used to come, often without prior notice, after big quarrels with her husband, a landlord with sprawling farms and hundreds of tenants. My aunt and uncle would fight over his getting concubines to produce an offspring, especially a son.

My aunt, unlike my mom, was not able to bear children. Whenever I overheard such stories, I used to think how unfair *ch'on-ji sihin-myong*, gods of heaven and earth, were. My sickly mom was having too many babies in quick succession, albeit daughters so far, while my more affluent and healthy aunt could not.

In early December of 1941, I noticed that whenever grown-ups got together, they talked in hushed voices as if something grave was happening. At the school, too, physical exercise classes changed. We started doing strange things, practicing to go up and down the stairs using only one side, scooting and staying down under the desks, and gathering in small groups and following the teachers to the darker interiors of buildings. I asked grown-ups what was going on, but they simply told me not to worry.

Shortly before the winter vacation in December, there was a big assembly of the whole school in the gymnasium. The principal and teachers were on the platform. Students were gathered in the order of grades, and separated by gender. Our lower-grade classes occupied the front rows. The principal went up to the lectern, ordered us to rise in attention, turn around to face the huge "Rising Sun" flag of Japan hung in the back top wall, and commanded us to raise our right hand to salute the flag. We then turned around to face the stage. The principal asked us this time to look to the east in the direction of the Japanese mainland and make deep bows to the Japanese emperor. After that, we were ordered to sit down.

Finally, the principal began with a loud, but unusually happy tone that we should all rejoice in big Japanese victory over the Western allied powers, first in annihilating American Pacific Fleet in Hawaii and in seizing Singapore. The whole hall erupted in loud applause. He motioned us to quiet down, and began.

"The Great Empire of Japan has been engaged in war against the Western 'devils,' Americans among them, who had been condescending toward us and had regarded us as inferior to them." He cleared his throat and continued.

"Our divine Emperor Hirohito could not tolerate such treatment any longer and had commanded that we lead *all* Asians under Japanese to demonstrate to the 'high-nosed' and 'yellow-haired' scoundrels that Asians would not tolerate their abuse." With the phrase, "high-nosed and yellow-haired" we chuckled, but he quickly quieted us, and went on.

"We will call this the principle of Greater Asia Co-Prosperity Sphere with Japan as its leader. The Great Empire of Japan under divine guidance has been winning battle after battle, and just 10 days ago, we conquered the city of Singapore, where the crucial product of rubber is produced. With the abundant supply of rubber in Japanese hands, the divine emperor's people will be victorious." And he started clapping hands himself. We all stood up, quickly followed suit, shouted loudly, and applauded. And at the same time, teachers took out big bulgy bags that had been hidden behind the screen, came down from the stage and handed out white rubber balls to students. We began cheering even louder. As we were dismissed we were told to make sure to show the balls to our parents and tell them what we had just heard from the principal.

My Father, Cho Pyong-chae (1909-1968), in Judge's Robe
as Pyongyang District Court Judge (1939-1943)

CHAPTER 5:

SOLO TRAIN RIDE

By the early months of 1943, Mom and Dad were openly discussing moving back to Seoul. I learned that Dad was often uncomfortable passing judgment on Koreans who were brought before him. Dad felt it was unfair to punish people for acts that he considered not so much as criminal offenses as expressions of frustration and Korean nationalism. He said that some days were more emotionally exhausting than others. One day, Dad dragged himself into the house after he returning home from work. As usual, Mom and I met him at the front door. We noticed that he looked tired and was dragging his feet. Mom asked him if he was sick.

"No, I am not," he answered, "but I just can't do this any more."

"What happened, Dad?" I asked.

"You are now nine years old, and you might as well know it too," he explained. "Today a middle-aged Korean fruit vender was brought to me for speaking rudely to a Japanese policeman. The Korean had placed his fruit basket on the side of the road. The Japanese policeman said it stuck out too far into the road, so he kicked it over, scattering the fruit. The Korean didn't even swear at him." Dad heaved a sigh. "But he got arrested and jailed anyway."

"Oh, my, can they do that?" Mom asked.

"They can do whatever they want with Koreans," Dad responded as he was taking his shoes off and putting on a pair of slippers. "They think they are superior to us. They have been ruling us almost thirty-three years and they are becoming cockier than ever. They treat us like animals." He sighed again as he started walking toward the main room.

From then on, Mom and Dad began talking seriously about returning to Seoul, including the matter of education of Cousin Soon and me. They decided to send me ahead of the rest of the family. I could be admitted to a reputable elementary school to finish the second semester of my second year. In that way, I would start the all-important third year as a returning student rather than a newly transferred kid. My cousin would return to his parents. They wanted him to stay with them for a semester, until we were resettled in Seoul.

One cold January morning, my parents put me on a train bound for Seoul, entrusted to a middle-aged train conductor. They made me promise that I would behave like a big girl and would not cry. I fought off tears and vigorously nodded my head. I don't remember what I did for three and a half hours alone on the train. The conductor came by frequently and checked on and asked me if I was all right. One time I heard him grumble after he came to see me, "What kind of parents would put a child that young on the train alone? Tse, Tse, Tse, poor thing traveling alone at that age!" When the train jerked to a stop, I found a blanket covering me from shoulder to the feet. *I must have fallen asleep. The conductor must have put this blanket on me. What a nice man.* As I was trying to get up from my seat, the conductor came over.

"We are in Seoul now, young lady," he said. "Hold onto my hand tightly. I will deliver you to your relatives in Seoul. I hope they are on time to meet you."

He walked fast past other passengers and got to a door. He got off first and stretched his hands out and motioned me to get off the steep metal steps of the train. He lifted me up, held my hand again, and looked around. The Seoul station was far larger and fancier than the Pyongyang depot. Lots of people were milling around. As the conductor helped me get down the steps, I saw Grandma a few steps away. I let go of his hand and ran toward her.

"Grandma-a-a-a!" I hollered at the top of my lungs.

Grandma walked fast toward me, followed by an uncle and a cousin. When Grandma reached me, she lifted me up.

Grandma made several deep bows to the conductor. "Thank you, sir," she said, "for taking such a good care of my granddaughter."

"Yes, Ma'am, but she was really no trouble," the conductor responded. "I was just worried that others might bother her. These are rough times, you know." I saw Grandma push a few *yen* into his pocket. He motioned to refuse the money, but he also had a big smile on his face.

Grandma held my face in the bowl of her hands and tenderly looked down at me.

"Bongwan-ah, *chongmal honja watne*, Bongwan, you really came alone!" she said. "I was so worried about you that I couldn't do anything all day today."

I breathed deeply and tears streamed down my cheeks.

"I am big now, you know," I replied. "See, Grandma?"

Grandma stroked my hair, held my hand and walked to an uncle, an aunt and a young male cousin, who were approaching us. I was so glad to see them.

"Oh, sure, sure, my little cousin girl," the boy laughed at me. "Sure, you are big alright, a big pretender. Look at her tears!" This was just a bit of mischief from my cousin Ikso, who was in his early teens. I learned later that he had a heart of gold and would get into fight with neighborhood boys to protect me, but in the house, he teased me a lot while I was living at Grandma's. This was the very first teasing. My oldest uncle, who was Ikso's father, scolded him.

"Shush, naughty boy!" Uncle said. "She is here alone without her parents. Be nice to her, you hear?"

Cousin Ikso stuck his tongue out at me. But then he winked and smiled at me. I didn't like the protruding tongue but like the winking eye, which indicated that he didn't really dislike me. Ikso was four years older than I.

Uncle hailed a couple of rickshaws. Grandma and I got into one and the rest got into the other. I laid my head on grandma's laps and fell asleep.

"We are here, wake up, Bongwan."

"Umm-m. Where, *Umma* (Mommy)?" I rubbed my eyes and looked around.

"*Umma* is not here, poor child," Grandma said gently.

"Oh yes, of course. I forgot," I said. "But you are here with me, *Halmoni*, Grandma."

"Yes, of course, my baby." Grandma hugged me.

I remembered that I was supposed to behave like a big girl. I stood up on the rickshaw floor steadying myself. Grandma quickly grabbed my hand, moved ahead of me and got off the vehicle first, reaching out to me. My oldest uncle quickly dashed over from the rear rickshaw and picked me up and put me down.

CHAPTER 6:

GRANDMA'S BIG HOUSE

When my uncle put me down from the rickshaw, I looked around and could see that we were at Grandma's big house. Fond memories flooded through me and temporarily helped me forget that I would have to live away from my parents for several months. I remembered when Mom and I used to come here before we moved to Pyongyang.

I was freshly struck by the size of the main gates. Perhaps even more now because our Western-style house in Pyongyang had only a small entryway. The main entrance consisted of huge two-sided varnished wooden doors with black wrought-iron hardware. In their center were big black iron half circles with black doorknocker rings, which perfectly matched each other when closed. On both sides of the shiny gates were tall varnished flat pillars with Chinese characters. Those on left pillar were Grandpa's name, "Ku Ch'ang-jo." The right pillar bore characters representing long life, prosperity and happiness.

After paying the rickshaw pullers, Uncle moved to the center of the locked gates and called loudly that we had arrived. From inside came a man's quivering voice, saying that he was coming immediately. As the two parts of the gate parted with a creaking sound, a slender middle-aged man emerged, bent his body low, and mumbled welcoming words.

"You should oil the hinges," Grandma said to the doorman.

"Yes, ma'am as soon as I can," he answered, bowing again.

Grandma and Uncle held my hands and lifted me up over the high threshold of the gates.

When I passed the second set of gates, a beautiful courtyard opened up in front of me. Inside, all was the way I remembered it. There was the island with its trees, bushes, rocks—yes, even the little waterfall. I had always loved visiting this big house and snooping around its many odd corners. I felt refreshed from a long train ride and relieved from the anxiety of traveling alone. I released my hands from those of Grandma's and Uncle's and sped around the island. The ground of the courtyard was covered with smooth gravel so it was easy to run. I raced with my both hands up and my head turned skyward. I even bellowed out cheering sounds. Adults hailed me on, but the cousins were murmuring, "Strange kid. Is she going to live here—for how long?"

The square courtyard was surrounded by multi-tiered structures on all sides, which were the apartments of various sizes for the married uncles and their families. Opposite the oldest uncle's apartment were the kitchen and the passageway to the backyard. The kitchen was like a cavern. On its floor of pounded earth was a stone platform holding three big iron cauldrons. The rice was cooked in the center pot, soup and vegetables in the other two. Ducts provided the heat for the pots. The heat for Grandma's *anbang* passed through the same ducts.

Next to the kitchen was the third uncle's place, at the end of which stood a gateway to *sarang ch'ae,* the outer sector, a complex of Grandfather's bedroom, a library, a guests' reception room, and an errand boy's room.

From the kitchen, I could go to the backyard, which was one of my favorite places in the house. It was a big sunny, open space of stamped dirt, surrounded by servants' apartments. At its center were clotheslines on bamboo poles. In one corner was a platform where numerous shiny earthen crocks were arranged neatly in rows according to their sizes. On the other corner were white wooden arches on which hung climbing vines of morning glories. The earthen jars were storage pots containing soy sauce, bean paste, hot paste, and *kimchi*. Next to it was a storage shed, or *kwang*, with two panel wooden doors with black steel hardware and an oversized lock.

Against its interior walls were rice and other grain sacks of rough straw stacked up high to the ceiling. Its matted dirt floor was covered with wooden planks in the middle, which covered the holes where clay jars for winter *kimchi* were buried. Behind these structures was an alley with funnel holes to heat rooms. A stonewall marked the end of the property. The thick wall had a roof of grey Korean tiles and was covered with grape vines and other vegetation.

Uncle carried my small satchel up the stairs to the *anbang*, where I was to stay for the next several months. As I was following Grandma, I looked back to the courtyard. My cousins looked aghast, for none of them were allowed to set their foot in that room, let alone sleep in it. The *anbang* was one of a few places in the house where children were not allowed, especially because it had a spacious attic, where grandmother stored a lot of her dry goods, bolts of fabrics of all kinds on one side and dried foods on the other, candies, rice cakes, honey, sweet rice drink among them.

I already missed my parents, but at the same time, I began to feel excited with the prospect of staying with Grandma in her *anbang*. I looked forward, as I used to when I visited the house before, to exploring many forbidden corners, sneaking into Grandpa's library and trying his ink stone and writing brushes, and getting covered with soot crawling through a low tunnel of heating flues. I was also excited about getting acquainted with my cousins, especially a girl cousin, who was my age. But I was worried about how to get along with the male cousins, especially the second of the three, Ikso, who came out to meet me at the railroad station but made a mean face and stuck his tongue out at me.

CHAPTER 7:

EELS AND ANTLERS

My parents moved back to Seoul in the summer of 1943 and I joined them after several months of staying at my grandparents' house. Nobody thought much about the significance of our move in that year, but it turned out to be a fortunate turn of events for our family. It was just two years before the Korean peninsula was "temporarily" divided between the North and South along the 38th parallel. Seoul was in the southern part and Pyongyang in the northern area, and the latter became the capital of the North.

Our new house, a big Korean-style house, was located on Tangju-dong, a fairly wide side street near the busy boulevard of Kwanghwa-ro, now called Sejong-ro. It was not as big as my Grandparents' house, but much bigger than our pre-Pyongyang home and closer to the center of the city.

Dad and Mom chose this location, I was told, for a few reasons: Dad wanted to situate his law office in its *sarang ch'ae*, outer part, which was separated from the *anch'ae*, the inner living quarter, with a big wooden gate; it was close to the Susong elementary, a choice school, to which I had been transferred prior to their relocation; and finally, it was big enough for a growing family, now with three daughters with a fourth child on the way, my cousin, a few household helpers, and two young male helpers for Dad's law practice.

By that time I had finished the first semester of the third grade in the new school with the first ranking in the class. A rare achievement, said the teacher. A shock, blathered my sassy Seoul classmates, who had been cold-shouldering me for having transferred from countryside. Granted, Pyongyang was the second-largest city, but it did not matter. Anywhere out of Seoul was considered inferior. I surprised everyone obviously, but the honor came at a high price. When the new fall semester was about to start, I felt indisposed but told no one, for fear that my parents would keep me home causing me to fall behind again. I had found that the academic level of the Pyongyang school was indeed lower and I had much catching up to do. But luckily, I thought, no one noticed that anything was wrong with me. Dad was preoccupied with launching his law practice, transforming a traditional Korean room in the *sarang ch'ae* into a Western-style office with a desk, a tufted leather swivel chair, and file cabinets. He also needed to re-establish a network of legal professionals after four years of absence from the capital. Mom was busy helping Dad as well as settling down in the new, old big house.

Within a month, however, I became too ill to conceal my condition. One afternoon just before dismissal, I fainted at school. Immediately, I was taken home and did not return to school for several months. Mom took me to her room and hid all my books and papers, and a young babysitter was assigned to me around the clock to report to the adults any of my foolish behaviors, such as reading, writing, and doing arithmetic. Having lost a child a few years earlier from misdiagnosis and noticing that I was too weak to travel, my parents called on several doctors to visit me at home. Three Western-medicine doctors agreed on a diagnosis that I had pleurisy, probably caused by exhaustion. They recommended absolute rest, good nutrition, and a pleasant mental attitude.

My mom set up a reclining bed for me in the middle of the *maru*, the center hall of the house. For Mom, who was a meticulous homemaker, this was a sacrifice. She had little tolerance for things misplaced around the house, and to have a bed in the middle of the *maru* must have been unthinkable, but I did not hear her complain. She just urged me to concentrate on getting better. I felt guilty, especially because she was so nice and that I, as the oldest, was causing her such trouble instead of helping her when she was trying to settle down in a new home.

Doctors and nurses of Western medicine came and went, but my condition did not improve dramatically. Grandma, who came to see me daily, became impatient with my slow progress. She pleaded with my parents to allow an herb doctor to visit me and told them that she could recommend a reputable one, who had miraculously cured a multitude of patients.

A long bearded middle-aged man in Korean attire came one early morning, which was supposed to be the most optimal time of the day for accurate diagnosis in Eastern medicine. The bearded man, who had no stethoscope, did not look like a doctor to me, but I had to let him hold my wrists to check my pulse, poke me under my jawbones, look into my mouth, and examine my tongue. Finally, when he put pressure on my right rib cage, I screamed.

"Aoo, ouch, that hurts."

"I guessed as much," he said, turning to Mom. "She still has liquid in the lining of the lung."

"I don't know what her condition was when she first got sick," he continued, "but the water has not been absorbed. I can prescribe some herbal medicine and also suggest that you prepare traditional nutritious brews of eels and stag antlers and have her drink it at least once a day."

"Eels and antlers, yuk." I said loudly. "I won't have them."

"Shush," Mom scolded me.

"Excuse me for her misbehavior," Mom apologized, bowing to the doctor. "I did not teach her properly."

I felt bad that I made her say "sorry" for no fault of her own.

"No problem," the doctor replied. "She's but a child. Please bear in mind though that she needs high potency nutritional stuff for a quick recovery."

In a couple of days, most of the Western medicine drugs were set aside, and I was supposed to imbibe brewed herbal medicine soup three times a day and an antler and eel concoction once a day. I dreaded the times when these brews were brought to me and I was thinking of pouring them outside in the backyard, but Mom or Grandma sat watch over me whenever I had to consume these yucky mixtures making it sure that not a drop was left in the utensils. Disgusting tasting as they were, they might have had some healing effect or the Oriental medicine might have boosted the Western treatment, which had started to work. At any rate, within a month or so, I felt stronger and begged my parents to send me back to school, but they turned a deaf ear to me. They allowed me only to go back to my own room with books and papers and to study at home.

I went to school after the winter break and found out that I had fallen behind. I plunged into studying non-stop and got sick again, this time much more seriously than before. I had to sit out the rest of the spring and summer, take the herbal medicine and antler and eel brews again. I had missed almost one half of each of the third and the fourth grades of elementary school. I returned to school at the end of the fourth grade. After that, I did not miss another day of school for the rest of my education in Korea.

Later years in my life, people often marveled at my health and energy, remarking that I functioned as if I had a nuclear cell in my body. I would quietly thank my parents' exhaustive care and give credit to those awful tasting cocktails of eels and antlers for my American nickname, "Energizer Bunny."

CHAPTER 8:

NAME CONVERSION

When I returned to school for the new academic year in early April of 1944, I noticed a few changes. Almost all of my classmates now had four-character names in the Japanese pattern. When the teacher called the roll, "Ayaki Tokuko, Okami Michiko," and then, "Cho Bongwan," my name now sounded odd although mine was the one unchanged. Everyone looked at me as though I was an alien with a strange name. Before I had left school, there were a few girls who had Japanese-style names, which sounded funny at the time. Now, the reverse had become the rule. Another new thing that caught my eye was over-sized placards in huge Japanese letters that said, "Japan and Korea are One" or "Inner (Japan) and outer (Korea) lands are one body." These posters now hung high on the walls everywhere.

The name conversion was one of many Japanese policies of complete cultural assimilation that attempted to transform Koreans (and other colonized people) into Japanese. Such policies had existed earlier but they were more systematically enforced after 1937. That was the year the Japanese imperial military instigated an armed clash with the Chinese Nationalist forces known as the "Marco Polo Bridge Incident" in the vicinity of Peiping (Beijing). This skirmish is considered to mark the beginning of the war between China and Japan (1937-1945) and the onset of World War II in Asia. Another of the assimilation programs was the exclusive use of the Japanese language outside our homes, enforcing it even on kindergarten children. The "logic" behind these stern rules was that by assuming Japanese names and speaking the language, Koreans and other colonials, would be treated as equals and not suffer from discriminations in education, employment, and government services, including that in the military. Koreans could now be drafted into the emperor's forces and have the honor to serve the divine emperor. In the beginning, the surname change was supposed to be voluntary, but its implementation became relentless when the tide of the Pacific war turned against Japan after 1943. Japan needed more troops to replace increasing casualties.

One afternoon, a few days after I resumed attending school, the teacher asked me to stay behind. I was nervous and was wondering what I had done wrong. While the teacher was getting organized at the end of the day, I went around the classroom to straighten out chairs, close the windows, and erase the blackboard. Finally, the teacher called me.

"Thank you for doing my job," she said. "You are indeed a nice girl," she added, beckoning me to come closer and sit down on a chair across her desk.

"This is nothing," I replied. "I do a lot more than that at home. I am the oldest and help out my mom a lot."

"Is that so? The teacher said. "You are really an exemplary girl, more so than I have known."

I bowed my head slightly to show appreciation. After a moment, she continued.

"Because you are such a good role model, it is important that your name should also be a name that suits your image and your good behavior."

"Thank you for the praise," I replied, startled. "But did you say my name doesn't suit me? How can't it? I've been called only by this name since my birth. Don't you like my name?" I was surprised to find myself talking so much to an adult.

"No, it's not that, but it's a Korean name. You have been a subject of the Japanese emperor all your life. It's about time your name should reflect that status."

"B—b," I sputtered. I wanted to say something, but before I had a chance, the teacher continued.

"I want you to go home and ask your parents, especially your father, to change the family name into Japanese style and give you a cute little Japanese girl's name, like Yoshiko or Chikako. Do you understand what I'm saying?"

"Yes, I understand." I nodded and lowered my head even further, not out of gratitude or respect but of irritation and worry. I did not like what I heard and already knew what my father's response would be.

I was familiar with the issue of the name conversion. We had to fill out the family register every month at the local police post. While I was entering the family record on my mom's behalf, my cousin Soon's name stood out. His name alone was in the four-character Japanese style. It was now Toyota Shiryu.

Toyota came from the name of the Cho clan's original geographical base, P'ung-yang. The letter "pung" was pronounced as "toyo" in Japanese and "ta" was added instead of "yang," which was pronounced, "yo" in Japanese. My dad and uncle thought that "ta" sounded better than "yo" after "Toyo" and that since both characters had the same meaning, "field," it was justified to use it. His given Japanese-style name was taken from his childhood name, "Ja-ryong," because he was born in the year of the dragon, which had the Japanese pronunciation of "Shiryu."

When I asked my parents why my cousin's name had been changed, my dad abruptly told me that it was to enable Soon to remain in school. His answer was so curt that I did not dare ask him to explain any further, but I remembered his mumbling about how long he could hold out and how long I would be left alone.

"So, the time has come," I said to myself as I was walking home listlessly. "They are not leaving me alone. But I won't say anything to Dad."

The fresh April air chilled my hot cheeks, which obviously had flushed while I was talking to the teacher.

I closed the large squeaky gate behind me and entered the inner quarters of our house, but I did not call out as usual that I was home. Mom heard the door, turned around and noticed my limp posture.

"Anything wrong, dear? You are later than usual."

"No, nothing. Just tired, very tired."

"You did not answer me. Why are you late?"

"I was talking to the teacher."

"About what?"

"Nothing." I dropped my voice. Mom stopped from setting the dinner table, walked over, held my cheeks in the cup of her palms, and looked me squarely in the eye.

"Bongwan, Teacher said something to you. What did she say? Have you done anything wrong? You have to tell me, or both of us, Dad and me. It's alright, we will listen to you."

"No, Mom. I didn't do anything wrong, but I don't want to talk about it now, at least not until Dad's available." I threw my knapsack on the edge of the *maru* and went into my room.

"Wake up, my daughter, I hear you want me." I heard my dad's voice. It was dark outside. I must have fallen asleep—the sleep of anguished exhaustion.

"Mom set a small table for you," Dad explained.

I had obviously slept soundly — through the dinner-time commotion of a large family.

"Just the three of us can sit and talk about whatever bothers you."

It was nice to have Mom and Dad all to myself, a rare occurrence. Either Mom prepared special dishes for me or I was so hungry that everything tasted especially good. Mom and Dad watched me eat and occasionally whispered among themselves. When I was almost done and taking the last gulp of water, Dad spoke.

"Mom told me that the teacher held you back and said something to you, but you won't tell her anything unless both of us are present. Here we are, my princess, now start. Whatever bothers you, you must tell us." The tenderness of Mom and Dad overwhelmed me—almost to tears.

"Dad, . . ." I hesitated.

"Go on," Dad urged me.

"The teacher, the teacher wants me to have different names and that you can and must change them."

"Do you want me to?" I shrugged my shoulders.

"Don't you like your name? I told you what your name means, and it's a good, respectable name."

"No, it's not that. I like my name although I get kidded that it sounds like a boy's. I am used to it now and want to keep it. But the teacher said you had to change our *surname*—to a two-character, multi-syllable Japanese family name as you changed Cousin Soon's and my given name to a cute little Japanese girl's name."

"My dear daughter, I'd do anything for you and you know that, but not this one." As expected, Dad did not mince words.

"I cannot change our family name that lasted 1,000 years because I have to perform *jesa,* ancestral ceremonies, for my father, and can't do it if I have a different name from his. I would be utterly un-filial not just to your grandfather but would dishonor the ancestors of the Cho clan." Dad took a sip of water and continued.

"Cousin Soon's case is different. He's my brother's son, and I am temporarily entrusted with his education. I could not take the risk of his having to interrupt his high school studies because of my stubbornness about keeping the family name. My brother and I had agreed that we had no choice because the Japanese authorities are expelling students without Japanese-style names. But you are still in the elementary level and even if you get ousted from and missed some school you can easily catch up as you are already doing after your prolonged illness."

This was the time when my father told me about the Cho clan's migration from China when the Jurchen and Khitan tribes conquered the northern half of the Song empire, reducing it to one half of its original territory. The surname, Cho, was the same as that of the ruling imperial Song dynasty's although he did not know how directly related we were to the main imperial line.

However justified, my father's refusal to accept name conversion for me had consequences back at school. Everyday thereafter, the teacher held me back after regular hours and ordered me to clean the classroom, putting the chair upside down on the desks, sweeping and mopping the floor. Knowing full well why the teacher was punishing me so, I did not disclose to my parents the reason for my late coming-home time. I told them that I was helping the teacher with grading exams and organizing papers, light, honorable tasks. I didn't want my father to be pressured into shaming his ancestors of long lineage. But the after-school punishment might have become a last straw. I succumbed to relapse. My extra efforts to catch up and after-hour's physical exertion was too much. By late spring, I became too weak to attend school.

But it did not matter. Now, American B-29 bombers flew over our heads with regular frequency and the bombing in Korea was supposed to begin soon as the Japanese mainland had already been bombed almost daily. All students in elementary school were forcibly evacuated in groups or asked to stay home. Young men, including high school students, were drafted into the military or into hard labor in the mines or munitions factories outside Korea, Manchuria, Hokkaido or Sakhalin. Cousin Soon's dad spent three days to travel from Kangnung and took his son home before the draft went into high gear.

I did not see my cousin for over a year. While I was recuperating during the same period, Dad urged me to review and improve my knowledge of the Korean alphabet, which he and Mom taught me earlier. He said I might need it sooner than later.

Jesa sang (ancestral ceremony table)

CHAPTER 9:
A LIBERATION BABY

The weather on August 15, 1945 was hot and humid even before noon. I had been standing in line for the rice ration since early in the morning. The distribution center, which was formerly a Korean-owned grain shop, was located across the street from the police depot, and the people, mostly Koreans, quietly waited in line under the watchful eyes of Japanese policemen. I had relieved Sunhee, an errand girl, several years older, who had been standing in line from before dawn. She needed to return to the house to help Mom with lunch.

I was wearing a new birthday dress that Mom made from a silky fabric of a lemon-green color, which she found after searching all over the city. Everything was in short supply and nice fabrics were no exception. It was the day I was turning eleven. I felt grown up and rather cocky, considering myself knowledgeable about a lot of things. As the oldest of a family of four daughters (two sons and a daughter were yet to arrive), I had often shouldered considerable responsibility, from babysitting to supervising homework for my younger sisters, to filling out family registers to running errands for Mom and Dad, often carrying important papers. On that day too, I was carrying a few sheets of essential documents on the family, which I had filled out and which were required for rice rationing.

The meager allotment of food had gone on for several months, and it had become increasingly difficult to get adequate amount of food for most families. In the past few months, our family of ten—two parents, four daughters, two maids for my mom, and two courier boys for my dad—never had enough to eat. But the lines at distribution stations were getting longer while the food ran out long before the lines ended.

I was feeling hungry, thirsty, and cross. *Why isn't Mom sending the girl back to relieve me? After all, it's, it's my b'. . .* I did not finish the sentence. I was ashamed that I even felt irritable just because it was my birthday. *The times are so bad, and I was supposed to be a "grown-up" girl after all. You shouldn't worry about a birthday!* I chastised myself.

Still, I was not feeling happy although I was now the fourth person from the front of the line. I looked down at the ground while alternating between reading the book that I brought and looking up to see whether my relief was coming. I moved ahead one more spot. I am now the third. *I need to have a satchel to put the rice in. Where is she?* It's now almost noon. The sun was beating down and my new dress was sticking to my back. I thought I should get ready. I dog-eared the page I was reading, took out the papers from the book's back cover, and straightened myself by smoothing my hair and dress. I heard the noon siren, which had been ringing every day, as long as I remembered. But I thought the siren was shorter that day than usual. *Well, they must have run out of electricity even to ring the siren long enough. It's already noon, I am getting closer to the front, and I don't have anything to carry the grain in.* Without realizing, I began stomping my feet. Then I heard Sunhee call out to me.

"*Kun Unni*, older sister," she cried. I turned around and saw her running toward me. I motioned to her to hurry up. She waved both her hands gesturing to call it off. I shrugged my shoulders. She was coming closer with the same hand gesture but with no container or satchel in her hand. When Sunhee finally reached me, I was the second in line. Before I had a chance to ask her why she did not bring any container, Sunhee grabbed me by my arms.

"*Appa* says to come home," she told me. "Don't worry about getting the rice from here." Sunhee called me "older sister" as my sisters did although she in fact was older than I was. She also referred to my mom and dad as *Umma* and *Appa* as we did. Sunhee had come to our house as an orphan when she was only eight years old, and my parents had sent her to elementary school. She did chores around the house, babysat, and ran errands.

"What? Are you sure?" I asked her, who was still out of breath. She briskly nodded her head.

"But why?" I complained. "I stood in line all these hours. I can't give up my place. I'm next." Impatiently, I brushed her hands off, clenched my fists, and stamped my feet to express my determination to keep my place.

"*Unni, Appa* said to tell you it's all over."

"What did he mean? What is 'all over'?"

"I don't know. He just said that and told me to go and get you without bothering to stay in line. He also has many friends. They are all sitting under the radio in dead silence listening to a grim voice."

"Listening to what?"

"I don't know. Please, *Unni*, let's go, OK?" She started pulling me by one arm.

People around us heard us. They began to gather around and asking us what was meant by "all over." The Japanese official who was doling out rice stared at us with a look of horror.

Sunhee and I brushed the others aside, broke away from the crowd and began running. In the distance we thought we heard thunders or roars of people.

I skipped over the two gates' thresholds and stepped inside the courtyard in front of the *maru*.

"*Appa*, did you tell Sunhee to come and get me? I was so clo . . ."

"Sheeee," A loud hushing sound stopped me. I looked around. What I saw stunned me. All the people looked as if they were frozen in space and time. Sitting under the radio, which was placed on a high shelf in the *maru*, were several of my dad's friends. Mom was sitting a few paces back with Grandma and an aunt. In the courtyard were all of our household helpers, all standing as if they came out in the middle of their chores. Only thing I could hear was a voice, a serious voice, as Sunhee said, coming out of the radio. I recognized it as the voice of the Japanese emperor from hearing daily imperial exhortations at school.

I turned to Sunhee, held her hand, and we stepped down two granite steps into the courtyard. Within a few minutes, the voice from the radio stopped. Everyone erupted into shouts and applause. Dad stood up and looked around.

"Is Bongwan here?" he asked.

"Yeh, *Appa*." I stepped over closer to the *maru*.

He ran down to the courtyard in his socks feet and lifted me up.

"You are my liberation baby! You are a good luck kid."

"*Appa*, put me down. I am not a baby. I am eleven years old." Dad lowered me.

"I guess you are right. You are not a baby any more, but you are my liberation baby just the same." He patted me on the head and then spoke to those around us.

"Everyone, look here," he exulted. "Here's my oldest kid. On her birthday, today, our country got liberated from Japanese Imperialists – after 35 long years. She's my kid and is my liberation baby indeed."

CHAPTER 10:
GHOSTS WALKING

After the giddy days following VJ Day in 1945, when I was adored as a "Liberation Baby," I had to settle down and go back to school. Returning to school after a long break was strange, the whole place somehow looked different. Stranger still was what was unfolding in the classrooms. I was assigned to an all-girls class of forty. We were speaking Korean. Out of habit, I looked around to see if anyone was spying on us for speaking our own language. Then, it occurred to me. *Oh, yeah, the Japanese are now gone and we are independent, hurray!* A joyous feeling soared from inside out. *Yes, we'll show them that we are not dumb as they tried to tell us.* I tightened my lips. There were other changes: the teachers were new, and there were several new students, who spoke in an accented Korean. Some came from China and others came from Japan. Those from the former were patriots' daughters; from the latter, children of collaborators. The two groups hardly spoke to each other.

A thirty-ish woman walked in and went to the front of the class behind the lectern and addressed us.

"*Haksaeng dul, joyong hae yo*, students, please be quiet." It sounded strange. It was not the usual greeting we were accustomed to. Another "oh yes" moment came to me —*no more Japanese teachers, who used to punish me for my family name*. We hushed each other and settled down. The lady continued.

"*Anyong haseyo*, hello. I am Teacher Yi, I will be your home-room teacher." She looked around smiling. She had a kind look and did not appear as stern as the Japanese teachers we had had. The teacher made a roll call, "Kim Ok-sun, Lee Jung-hee, Cho Bong-wan . . . " The names were no longer in Japanese style and my name fit in perfectly. *Oh, this is how it should be. Our family survived without changing our name.* I sighed a sigh of relief. I quietly thanked Dad for standing his ground.

"Does anyone among you know how to write "our country" and your name in *han'gul*, our Korean alphabet?" the teacher asked. I raised my hand high anticipating many hands up, but when I looked around, I was surprised. There were no other hands raised. *No one else knows han'gul? No other parents taught it to them?* I thought all kids spoke Korean and learned *han'gul* at home. But no one else knew how to write Korean letters. *Did Dad know this was going to happen?* I remembered what Dad said fifteen months earlier, "Study *han'gul*, you're going to need it sooner than later."

Thanks to my parents' foresight or patriotism in not losing our native language, I had a head start in classes conducted in Korean. With my health fully restored, I was able to charge ahead full-steam although still fully aware of the earth shattering changes occurring around me.

One day when I returned from school and stepped into our courtyard, I was so surprised that I almost fell backwards. The yard was full of half-naked, ghost-like figures, whom Dad's courier and errand boys were hosing and scrubbing down at the water pump. Another group of cleaner, but still skin-and-bone thin men filled the *maru* and were gobbling down food. Mom and the kitchen maids were running in and out of the kitchen carrying big trays laden with *tubu* soup, rice, *galbi*, short ribs, and *kimchi*. Dad and a few men were busily engaged in some serious conversation while watching over the whole scene. Our yard looked like an outdoor eatery with baths.

I later learned that these walking skeletons were political prisoners released from the infamous Sodaemun (West Gate) Prison, where they had been held for months and years, tortured, forced to do hard labor, and starved. When the Korean Bastille Day came, many of the prisoners had family and friends waiting for them, but even more of these men neither knew where to go, nor were they able to go due to their extremely weakened physical condition.

Dad had turned our home into one of the first half-way houses for the former prisoners, where they were cleaned up, given clean clothes, fed their first meals, helped to make connections with relatives and friends, and then sent on their way. Some of them were so weak that even I had to help out after school to spoon-feed them. Their images stayed with me even while I was at school. I could not concentrate on my studies and at night I had nightmares. Our house was in chaos. Former prisoners occupied every room, except three rooms for our immediate family. Male helpers had to share their rooms with them. Even Dad's office spaces were used as temporary bedrooms.

Mom was six months pregnant but was still working nonstop making huge batches of food. She had a few cooks to assist her, but it was she who oversaw all matters related to providing nutrition. She was overwhelmed and exhausted. At one of the dinner preparations, she was cutting beef ribs with a butcher knife while giving instructions to maids and she did not see her left middle finger was in the way. As she was splitting the ribs with the butcher knife in her right hand, she cut her finger with the same force as she was applying to the ribs.

A surgeon sewed together the severed ends of her middle finger but the center knuckle was so shattered that he had to remove it. Her left middle finger remained one knuckle shorter for the rest of her life.

The accident devastated my father. I heard Dad apologizing to Mom many times. Mom wept and said it was all right. She told him he was being compassionate and doing what had to be done. That evening as I was passing my parents' room, I overheard them talking.

"So, why not you?" she asked rhetorically. "Somebody had to do it! I have known that you would be the kind of person who would do difficult tasks nobody wants."

"But I underestimated the enormity of the task," Dad responded. "I should have known something like this couldn't be done at a private home. I am so sorry."

Dad's voice expressed his deep, sincere regret. I could hear that he was sobbing.

He immediately moved the prisoner aid camp to some other location. Mom's disfigured finger healed eventually. Her shorter middle finger dangled and moved about as if it was made of rag. But her overall health improved and in early December, she gave birth to a long-awaited son, Yun-song, the first since the death of Brother Tonsung several years earlier. It was twenty-two months after the fourth daughter, You-shin, was born in February of the previous year. I became "a little mother" to my baby sister, who had to give up Mom to the new-born brother.

CHAPTER 11:

A NATIONALIST

After the departure of the prisoners, our house felt empty but calm. By contrast, the school was operating in high gear. We were busy learning all things Korean—from the nation's founding myths to its current foreign relations. This included our Korean language, history, and geography.

It was during this lull in our family life, before the arrival of the new baby, that my father served as secretary of transportation for the United States Army Military Government in Korea (USAMGIK). From September 1945 until August 15, 1948, the Americans governed the southern part of the Korean Peninsula. The Soviet troops, who had only to cross into Korea from Manchuria following the Japanese surrender, were already in control of the north when the Americans arrived from their distant bases on the Japanese island of Okinawa.

What the Americans thought they knew about Korea they had learned from an extremely biased source: Japanese officials full of anger and shame over their defeat. According to them, Koreans were dirty, ignorant, uncivilized communists. This last claim fed American postwar fears of Communism. The sad irony was that Americans trusted their former enemies more than the people they were liberating.

It was in this hostile environment that my father became part of the American military government. The Koreans themselves had established a large number of political, cultural, and religious organizations. The Americans now issued orders to disband all existing Korean organizations, including the Korean People's Republic, founded by Yo Un-hyong (a.k.a. Lyuh Woon-hyung), an independent and left-of-the center nationalist. Yo was not invited to greet the American troops publicly at Inch'on. He soon became relegated into the "left block."

As the American military government was organized at the time, my father was the junior of the two secretaries to the ministry of transportation, the senior secretary being an American. Koreans were brought into the administration in order to present an appearance of a joint American-Korean rule; but in reality, Korans had little power. I heard my father talking to Mom that he had absolutely no authority to propose or make any decisions. All he was doing—hour after hour, day after day—was sitting at his desk to "rubber-stamp" decisions

Americans had already made. In less than three months he resigned the post. He did not want to be a robot, he told us.

People were surprised once again and gossiped as the time when he had resigned the judgeship in Pyongyang. To voluntarily leave as coveted a post as serving in the new government in Korea—whether it was a foreign military government or not—one simply did not do such a thing. Everyone was clamoring and even offering bribes to gain such posts. And here was a man who was voluntarily quitting. Something had to be wrong. Maybe he was "pink."

At about the same time, a law journal published an article that Dad had submitted a few months earlier. His article lamented that Korea was under another alien rule, this time, the American military regime. Although the American military government was new and supposedly democratic, Dad concluded, it was still a *foreign* government ruling Koreans. Every word was true. There was no denying that Americans were imposing a non-Korean authority. However, comparing them to the previous oppressive colonial government was still reprehensible. My father was severely criticized in newspapers and magazines. He and our house were under surveillance.

In the meantime, trumped-up charges were brought against Dad. For having held the position of a judge in the Japanese colonial government, he was labeled a collaborator, an unforgivable sin for Koreans after the war. It mattered little that he had resigned after a short time to protest Japanese treatment of Koreans. Dad was also accused of having Japanese friends and hidden Japanese property. One of his Japanese colleagues, a former judge, had asked him to keep a family heirloom, a wedding *obi*, or sash, that his wife had worn when they were married in Korea. The sash had only a sentimental value, and Dad had no idea if he would ever be able to return it to its owners.

The most damning charge against my father was that he had the insolence to criticize the American military government and had resigned a position in it. In the chaos of post-colonial Korea, there was no middle ground. One could not be a nationalist intellectual—either you were a blind follower of the new American regime or a leftist. There were plenty of highly learned Korean nationalists, who lamented the political division of the country, ideological rift among the educated, and establishment of yet another foreign power ruling over Korea. The difference was that my father had the audacity to speak up while few others had.

At dawn of one late February day in 1946, I was rudely awakened by a commotion in our yard. I opened the sliding door of my bedroom and peeked out. What I saw knocked me over. My father was being handcuffed and led away by uniformed policemen and Mom was running behind him screaming. I dashed out and joined Mom trailing after the departing group. But it was no use. Dad was already outside the gate and carried away in the open back of a small truck without any overcoat or blanket in the cold February dawn. He was visibly shivering but still nodded at us with a forced smile and was saying something. We could not hear him, but by his looks I could tell he was trying to comfort us.

Through the winter morning air, Mom's cries echoed:

"You can't do this. Bring back my husband. He did nothing wrong. He was only being upright and honest." I put my hand on Mom's back and attempted to calm her. Her upper body bobbed up and down from sobbing. I gently led her inside the house.

For the next few years, my father was taken into custody twice a year, shortly before and after March 1 and August 15. The former was the March First Independence Movement Day, a national holiday, to commemorate the largest scale anti-colonial uprising in 1919, and the latter was the VJ day as well as the founding day of the Republic of Korea (ROK), a separate south Korean government. The authorities had feared that my father would become a leader or a focal point of anti-government demonstrations.

I missed my father on my birthday, August 15th, during my early teen years.

CHAPTER 12:

AWAKENING

I grew up fast for the next few years while helplessly watching Father dragged out in handcuffs twice a year. It would be usually at dawn a few days before March 1st and August 15th of every year. Mom figured out the exact date when the authorities would come, would get up early, and fix some light breakfast for my father, and I would get up to help her. But Dad would only drink some soup and hardly touch anything else. Mom and I would both be on the verge of tears, but Dad was always trying to put on a cheerful face and comfort us.

"It will only be a week—now I know," he would say turning to Mom. "Make sure you take a good care of the children and manage the household helpers, including my courier boys, while I am gone." Mom would nod with her head turned away from Dad trying to fight her tears. My father would then face me and continue.

"You are my oldest and a reliable kid. I know you will look after Mom and your siblings, right?"

"Yes, of course, *Appa*," I would answer in a forced cheerful voice. "Don't worry about us. You take a good care of yourself. Eat even if you don't like the food they give you, promise?"

"Yes, my young lady," Dad replied. "I promise."

As he was leaving the house, he would turn around, give us a smile and motion with his manacled hands for us to go in. But I would stay out and watch him lifted onto the open back of a pick-up truck, where crouched were several other men who had been similarly rounded up.

As I followed Mom into the house, tears would stream down my cheeks, tears of sadness, anger, betrayal, and endless questions. *Why, why? What has he done? He was an anti-Japanese nationalist, upright and honest.* In those moments, I felt the awakening of an adult moral awareness in me. I strove to discern right and wrong and to understand why the world was full of evil and injustice. This world was the space outside our family and home, whose existence I had not known before. But now, there was this area, bigger and wider than my parents' home, and this outer world appeared to be in turmoil. I was not sure of its condition in terms of the balance between the fairness and unfairness. From the chaotic state of affairs in our society at the time, I was uncertain if the equilibrium would ever be restored. I was worried about the future of the newly liberated Korea.

I was also beginning to realize that I was having ideas of my own, not exactly in harmony with my parents ideas,' especially those of my mother. I became critical of Mom after she had two more babies—another son, Iksong, and *yet another* daughter, Sungsun, — in 1947 and 1949. She was frequently complaining that she was continually exhausted and worried about how to give proper care to all of us, now altogether seven. I debated for a while but dared to talk to her one day about why she kept having children if she was so tired. People had large families at the time perhaps due to the lack of knowledge of birth control. She was horrified. Her good little daughter dared to question her actions. But I did not regret that I conveyed my opinion to her. I remember that this was the first time that I was openly critical of my mother.

I noticed that Dad's income was dwindling due to the fact that his law practice was declining because of his twice-yearly imprisonments. Obviously, few people sought legal advice from a man who was so often in trouble himself. Even with interruptions, my father maintained his law office and our lifestyle, as if nothing had changed. I thought this was unwise although I did not say anything to my parents.

Nobody knew what I was going through or what changes were occurring in my thoughts. I was still just a twelve-year-old going on thirteen, now in excellent health, with a cheerful appearance, never missing a day of school, and getting good grades. Few outside my family knew about turmoil at our home: Dad's sufferings as a political dissident, our ever-growing family, and my extra responsibilities as a back-up mom for my fourth sister. Mom was doting on the long-awaited baby boy so much that the rest of us were left to ourselves, to the cook, the babysitter, and the errand boys. And I was taking on more responsibilities, for the household helpers were not able to relieve me from being a "little mother" to Youshin, my youngest sister then. As soon as I returned from school, she would run and cling to me and would not let go of me until her bedtime. Many days, I had no choice but to put off doing homework until after my "little mother" role was done.

When examination times came, I resolved that there was no way that I could get studying done at home. Although I felt ruthless doing so, I told Mom I had to go to the city library. She reluctantly agreed. I would leave the house at dawn before the library opened to make sure I got in and found a seat. I would study all day until the library closed. After returning home, I would have late supper, fight sleepiness, and stay up to review what I studied during the day—often until midnight. I could have gone to sleep two hours earlier, but I persevered. I remember now why I persisted. Around that time, a nagging thought crept into my mind, giving me a sense of being "awakened" to the fact that I was not, and never had been, a genius as people had been calling me. *How ridiculous for them to think that I was a genius! They don't know what real geniuses are like.*

I am not, definitely not, one of them! Another insight that occurred to me then was that I had reached an age when innate intelligence alone was insufficient to maintain high achievement level. *The conclusion,* I thought, *was work hard, because there was no getting away from it.*

In 1947, I was second in the class of two hundred when I graduated from the Susong Elementary School. I missed being the first by a slim margin, and I was not happy. But my parents showered me with praises for having done well despite my long absences in the third and fourth grades. I was admitted to Kyunggi Girls' Middle School, my mother's *alma mater*, and one of the most prestigious schools for girls at the time. I remember my parents' debating and arguing about which middle school they should send me. Father's choice was Ewha Girls' Middle School, the first modern school for girls in Korea, which was established by American Methodist missionaries in 1886. Ewha was just as high caliber as Kyunggi but was regarded a notch below in the eyes of the established Korean elite. It had the reputation of having a freer atmosphere of learning and much less structured system of education. Dad had attended Ewha's counterpart boys' school, Paejae, founded by American Presbyterian missionaries two years before Ewha. In the end, Dad deferred to Mom not just because Kyunggi was Mom's *alma mater* but also because Mom's reasoning made sense that parents simply should not deprive of a child's accomplishment of getting admitted to a school such as Kyunggi. But my father worried about my being in Kyunggi because its principal was the wife of one of the most conservative politicians, one of his political foes.

I did notice sharp stares and no smiles from the principal whenever I happened to run into her in the hallways and staircases although I was never called to her office. I plugged along heedlessly and turned out to be a star student, placing in the top one percent of every class I was in, excelling in all fields except in sports, including arts and crafts. I won the first prize in a national calligraphy contest, and I wrote for posters and placards of the school's rules and regulations, admonitions, and wise sayings that were hung around the school building. My embroidered cushion cover garnered an award and was exhibited at a prominent spot at a school bazaar.

Three years later in 1950, when I finished the year, I was the first of the graduating class and promoted to the upper school, Kyunggi Girls' High School. The principal did not smile at me as she was handing me the first place certificate.

By this time, my father was cleared of all his past "sins" and was no longer harassed. He relocated his law office to one of the office buildings flanking the city hall plaza, a premier location, and was beginning to revive his weakened law practice. His prestige as an independent-thinking intellectual was further enhanced when the American Military Government appointed him as a member of the Korean observer group to the U.S.-Soviet Joint Commission of 1946 and 1947. My mother's taxi business, which she started a couple of years earlier to supplement Dad's declining income, was flourishing after a fledgling start. My parents now had two sons, Yun-song and Iksong, one more than they had wished for, and five daughters, myself, Bongsoon, Ugza, Youshin, and Sungsun. I was admitted to the top-tier high school and the rest of my siblings were healthy and flourishing. Our house regained substance as well as appearance of a large, successful prosperous family living in a big traditional Korean house in the center of Seoul.

Little did I know that black clouds were fast approaching, bringing convulsive and violent storm, which would turn our world upside down to the scale that I had never imagined possible. The Korean War broke out on June 25, 1950.

A middle school class photo of 1948
I am the second from the left of the first row.

CHAPTER 13:

THE OUTBREAK OF THE WAR

June 25, 1950 was a beautiful Sunday. The school year was almost over and my middle school years too. Although there was no graduation ritual, it was obviously a milestone to move to the high school in the fall. My parents decided to treat us for having done well in the past school year by sending my two sisters, Bongsoon and Ugza, and me to a concert. Since I was fifteen going on sixteen and our house was close to the main thoroughfare, they let us walk to the concert hall located on Sejong-Ro. I had no problem with that. Three of us held hands, I in the middle, walked and skipped and reached the music hall in no time at all.

I don't remember exactly what the music program was although I recall that it was a classical symphony concert and when I think about the day, somehow

Dvorak's *New World* comes to mind, and it is the favorite piece of mine as well as Korean people. I could not pay much attention to the music, for I was pre-occupied with keeping my eleven and nine year-old sisters sit still. The concert lasted about an hour and a half. When we came out of the music hall, it was late afternoon, I had no watch but guessed that it was around 4:30 and 5 p.m., but the summer day was still bright and cool breezes felt good on our cheeks coming out of the stuffy music hall with no air-conditioning.

As we were walking down the steps and looking ahead to the plaza in front, we noticed that a large throng of people had gathered in front of the column billboard in the middle. I held my two sisters' hands tightly and ran to it to see what was going on. I saw that people, who had a chance to see what's on the board, would dash out of the crowd as quickly as they could, mumbling something like "Oh my god, we are in a big trouble." I plied through three or four people thick ring and reached the billboard, tip-toed to read the top part and quickly read down. A chill ran through my body. I grabbed my sister's hands, tore out of the crowd, and ran as fast as I could in the direction of our house. My sisters were bewildered. As they were following me, out of breath and panting, they were pulling my hands and asking me,

"*Unni, owe gurae,* Sister, why are you doing this?" I told them to run just as fast as they could. I told them we had to get home as quickly as we could manage. But they did not stop asking me. All the while I literally pull them without bothering to answer them. Bongsoon, the older of the two pouted, stopped running, and said,

"If you don't tell me, I am not going to run." She plumped down on the street.

"Ok, ok, but you will be scared, I warn you. I wanted Mom and Dad to tell you, but you leave me no choice." I heaved a breath, pulled up Bongsoon from the street, and looked them both in the eye and said.

"A war broke out."

"What?" My two sisters stopped and looked at me wide-eyed.

"A war? What does that mean? Are we going to die?"

"No, no, that's why we have to get home to Mom and Dad. The In-min Gun, North Korean People's Army, crossed the 38th parallel." They did not quite understand.

"What's the 38th parallel?"

"Dad will tell us. Let's hurry. We have to get home, hurry." I held onto their hands tighter and we ran faster.

"*Umma, uri watsoyo*, Mom, we are home." I screamed as we entered our house.

"*In-min Gun ni ch'o duro watte.* The People's Army invaded us." I bellowed out.

"*Anda, anda*, I know, I know. *Aigoo, naesekki dul ah*, Oh, my babies, you are home! I am so glad you are safe." She ran down from the *maru* hugged us all three in a big sweeping motion. A sense of warmth and security ran through my body. *Oh, I brought my younger sisters safely home and we are fine.* I breathed a deep sigh of relief.

"It's almost supper time. Go wash up and let's have something to eat, and *Appa* will tell us what's going on, OK?" Mom said to us. We nodded and I led my sisters up the steps to the *maru* and our rooms.

Dad explained to us. The In-min Gun, the people's army of the North, had indeed crossed over the border that divided the North and South but he also assured us he would do anything to protect us.

"But *Appa*, I thought the line was temporary, and I didn't know it had become like a border between the two different countries. Isn't Korea one country?" I asked.

"Yes, I am surprised you know about it. It's a long story, but to put it simply, the 'temporary' became 'permanent' since the separate governments were established in the North and South two years ago in 1948." Dad started explaining further. My younger siblings had finished the supper and Mom sent them off with a baby sitter to get ready for bed. Mom and I stayed to hear about Dad's analyses of how the situation had deteriorated to the outbreak of a war between the two Koreas: many failed attempts to erase the demarcation line, including the US-USSR Joint Commission in the spring 1946 of 1947 in which he was an observer; mounting suspicion on both sides; unceasing rhetoric from both sides to unify the land one way or the other; the North's refusal to admit U.N. election observer group; and failure of prominent nationalists' effort to persuade Kim Il-Sung.

I could tell Father was becoming upset and emotional as he was describing to Mom and me what had been happening to Korea.

"Only if they, Dr. Syng-man Rhee in the South and Kim Il-sung in the North, could have set aside their political ambitions and thought about the long-term future of the country . . ." Then, he quickly added.

"But it's not just their fault. It's Korea's location, and it's because we are where we are."

"What do you mean, Dad?" I asked. Dad's explanation continued.

The Korean peninsula was situated so strategically and surrounded by the big countries that none of the Powers wanted to give it up to others. After WWII, the United States and Soviet Union were leading the two hostile Communist and non-Communist blocs. The soviets supported Kim Il-sung and the U.S. Syngman Rhee.

With tacit consent of the two super powers, the two governments were established in Korea: the Republic of Korea (ROK) in the South on August 15, 1945, and three weeks later on September 9, the Democratic People's Republic of Korea (DPRK) in the North. Dr. Syngman Rhee, an American-educated septuagenarian, became the first president of South Korea, and Kim Il-Sung, the Chairman of the Korean Workers Party and president of the country.

Almost as soon as the two separate governments were established, the two leaders started talking about unifying the country – on their own terms.

"These two guys, Rhee and Kim, wished to be the unifier and never stopped talking about it." Dad resumed.

For President Syngman Rhee, however, it was mostly an empty rhetoric, for he had not received significant military assistance from America. For Kim Il-Sung, it was a different story. In addition to having on hand tens of thousands of battle-tested young Koreans who returned from China in late 1949 after years of fighting in the Chinese civil war, he was encouraged by what American Secretary State, Dean Acheson, did *not* say. Acheson did not include Korea in America's Asian defense perimeter in his policy speech at the National Press Club on January 12, 1950. With acquiescence from Stalin and Mao Tse-tung, Kim Il-sung amassed his forces all along the 38th parallel in preparation for his troops to cross the border at 3-4 a.m. on June 25, 1950. The attack was so unexpected that even President Rhee did not know about it until three hours later, and the general public not until the afternoon. By the evening, we heard the sound of cannon, first from distance and then closer and closer.

For the next three days we huddled under the radio hung high on the wall in the *maru* while wearingly cognizant of sound of guns getting louder. On the third day, we heard a huge explosive sound coming from the southerly direction. Mom sent out an errand boy to find out what was going on. He came back running and told us that the bridge on the Han River was blown off. The quivering voice of President Syngman Rhee came on the radio, assuring us that he would stay on to protect the capital and that we the people should do the same and should go about business as usual. We would soon learn that the announcement was a recording and that he and his government had already left Seoul and destroyed the bridge on the Han River to prevent the People's Army from pursuing him.

That same night, armed robbers broke into our house, tied up my parents, pointed a gun at them, put us children to the corner with a gunned guard watching us, and ordered our cook to show them where the rice and other grains were. They took all our provisions without leaving a single sack of rice except a small bag on a kitchen shelf, which they missed.

The war and hard times are upon us. What are we going to do? The situation was bleak indeed, but what I did not realize was that this was just the beginning. Greater hardship would await us and I, as a small-sized mid-teen kid, would play multiple roles, running errands for quick grocery shopping and going downtown to Dad's law office to pick up and deliver papers to his close associates. I would skip over bombed corpses and building debris in the city. I tried to put on an innocent smiley face of a little girl but I was scared to the core of my guts. I was beginning to face situations never imagined in my short life.

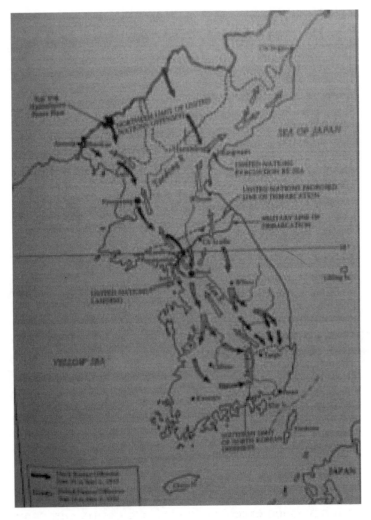

North Korean invasion, June 25, 1950
Andrew C. Nahm, History of the Korean People, p. 375

CHAPTER 14:

YOUTH VOLUNTEER CORPS

After the armed robbery, our large family experienced extreme shortage of food. My parents trimmed the household staff. Mother let the cook go, and that was not a difficult dismissal because the woman wanted to be with her son's family during the crisis. Mom now had only a young babysitter, and I filled in to help her with food preparation, taking care of my infant sister and other younger siblings, and general household chores. Since Father's law practice basically stopped, he released courier boys and only kept a younger errand boy who doubled up to help him and do other work around the house. Even then, we had little food in the house and could not even buy much except at an exorbitant price. Our daily meals consisted of cooked mixed grains and watery soybean sprout soup. There was hardly any protein in any food we ate because meat was hardly available, and even *tubu* (tofu) as vegetable protein was scarce. We were always hungry. My young brothers and sisters constantly whined that they were starving. Often times, I pretended that I was not hungry and let much of my portion to my younger siblings.

Everyone's nerve was frayed. Kids were crying or grumbling, Mom and I were overworked, and Dad was anxious. It was in this kind of atmosphere that I got into an argument with Mom one day at the breakfast table. I don't remember what and how it got started. All I remember was that I was blamed, as I had been lately, for my younger siblings' misdeeds. Up until that time, I took Mom's reproach as I was supposed to as the oldest, but that morning, I felt that I had enough of unjustified denunciations from Mom. Without talking back to Mom, which I was prohibited from doing and had never done, I just got up and bolted out of the house and ran in the direction of the school. About a half way through on the road, I realized that the North Koreans and their sympathizers had taken over the school and we had secretly been warned not to come to school although it was open. But after leaving the way I did, my pride in the family was at stake. I decided that I could not turn back.

When I reached the school, I was surprised that it was quite full. The first hour routine was normal. In the second hour, however, a loud speaker blared through the campus ordering us to assemble in the auditorium. Seeing the North Korean flag hung on the stage wall, my heart sank and the feeling crept into my mind that I was at the wrong place and at the wrong time, but it was too late. Surrounding the students and standing along the all were North Korean uniformed guards and dourly dressed mostly new men and women teachers although a few faces I recognized. Speeches began. Person after person lectured us how we should be grateful because the North Koreans liberated us from the tyranny of American puppet, Syngman Rhee, and American imperialists. Monotonous harangue went on and on. It was approaching mid-day and my stomach was growling. I had left the house without even drinking the watery soup. Then, we were lined up and marched out of the school ground. In the front, a man and woman in North Korean military uniform carried a sign, "Youth Volunteer Corps." Although we were herded into forming a marching group and forced to follow the leader, we were supposed to have "volunteered." When I realized what was happening and looked for ways of getting out, I could find none. We were completely surrounded by soldiers and adults with red banners across their chests and holding small North Korean flags. We walked what seemed to me like an eternity, listening and coerced into "singing," repeating and mumbling after the lead singer, the North Korean military marching song.

After about an hour of fast march, we arrived at the campus of a boys' boarding high school toward the northern edge of the city. We entered the two-sided metal gate with peeling light green paint. The gates were promptly closed and locked up with a huge black metal lock. The fully fenced in schoolyard was full of people, students and adult men and fewer number of women. Boys of our age were standing around at one end of the enclosure, and they were watched over by uniformed and plain clothed adults. After head counts, our group was led to the second floor, where there were small dorm rooms. We were assigned two to a room, told to wash up and reassemble on the first floor for lunch. *On my God, we are captives. They forced us to march here. I am supposed to live here and for how long? I didn't mean not to return home—just wanted to get away a while to make Mom realize that she was unfair. This is not what I intended. Am I going to be taken to the battleground or to the North? Am I not going to see Mom and Dad forever? I am so sorry, Mom and Dad, I should not have left home.* Fear and anxiety gripped me, almost paralyzing me. I plumped down on the squeaky bare bed and cried. I forgot all about how hungry I was.

Maybe it was the third day, while we were in drill in the yard, we heard commotions outside the high fence with barbed wire on top. Ignoring warnings from the loud speaker, we all ran to it. There were parents and relatives of some of us. They were tiptoeing and jumping up and down to catch a glimpse of us. Then, I heard, "Ma'am, I see Bongwan." "Where, where? Where is my daughter?" Suddenly, I heard my mom's voice. I ran to the spot. The errand boy was raising mom, and I could see Mom's teary face above the barbed wire of the fence.

"Only late yesterday we found out where you were, and we came as quickly as we could. Dad is working to get you out." Mom told me in hushed voice.

"When?"

"Soon."

"*Umma, chalmot hatso yo*, Mom, I did wrong, I am sorry." I started wailing with tears streaming down my cheeks.

There was loud yelling behind us to come away from the fence. Each one of us was forcibly pulled down and people outside were ordered to leave immediately.

The next day, I was called to step outside the classroom where we were learning about Kim Il-sung's heroic patriotism in Manchuria during the colonial period. A grimly dressed woman yanked my hand and led me outside. I saw my father, accompanied by the errand boy, was standing below the granite staircase. I ran to him, buried my head and cried.

"Let's get out of here before they change their mind." Dad firmly held my hand, and he and I followed the fast-walking errand boy toward the guarded gate. Dad showed them some kind of papers, and they reluctantly opened the green metal gate barely enough for us to squeeze through and let us out.

To this day, I don't know if my father bargained my freedom with his or not. But a few days after I got home, one of Dad's former colleagues, a close friend before the division, who had gone to the North, came with a few

In-min Gun soldiers and hustled my father out. When Mom asked him where he was taking Dad, he simply said, he wanted to have a friendly visit and a chat after a long interval. After all, they were such good friends before the partition. He said she should not worry. He would not keep Dad too long. As they were escorting him out of our house, Mom and I exchanged a look, look of suspicion and concern.

Dad did not come home that evening, nor the next day and day after.

Early on the third day, Mother sent out the errand boy where Dad's friend was staying. As soon as she found out, she left the house in search of my father. She carried a bag loaded with gifts with some of her treasured jewelry, celadon-glaze vases, and a few bolts of silk. She was gone most of the day. When she returned, she was exhausted and pale despite the hot and humid mid-July weather. When I pursued her, she told me that they had taken him into custody, preliminary to persuade him to go north for they needed talents like my father's.

"What if Dad refuses to go?" I asked.

"Then, I guess they will force him."

"You mean kidnap him?"

"I guess that's the word." Mom responded.

"Like my friend's dad?"

"Don't say that. I don't want to hear the word. I won't let that happen." Mom said.

"Listen, Bongwan. I will be going there every day from dawn to dusk and camp out until they let your father come home with me. You are really going to be the 'mother,' not so little any more. You must take a good care of your younger brothers and sisters while I am gone. Do you hear me? No more running away from home!"

"Yes, Mom. I wouldn't think of leaving home, especially without you. Just bring Dad home." I bowed my head, out of remorse and determination to do a good job during her absence. I just prayed that she would succeed in her effort to bring Dad home.

For the next two weeks, I saw Mom leaving the house when it was still dark and did not return until after dark. She told me one day that she was simply squatting in front of the house where my father was under "house arrest." She also let my father's former friend know that she was not taking any food except for water. My mom, a slightly built person, was losing weight.

I heard later that Dad's friend was moved by my mother's dedication and perseverance and released my father, saying there was no use having a man who had no passion for the North. The North Korea was full of people with burning desire to build a super nation. I suspected that he did not want to have an adverse publicity on endangering a woman's life by ignoring her "hunger strike" while they were trying to warm up to South Koreans under occupation.

In the meantime, I was notified that I was expelled from Kyunggi high school. I had no school to attend when the school opened late – in the middle of September after

General Douglas MacArthur led his famous X Corps to land at Inch'on harbor and liberated Seoul. I ended up "skipping" the 10th grade. I often despaired of what my future held, but most of the time, I did not lose hope that I would go to some school sometime soon and would eventually go to college. I was confident that my father would not spare his resources to find a school for me. With my parents' help, I got all the books for my grade and beyond, and I studied more diligently than ever.

CHAPTER 15:

LIFE UNDER THE NORTH KOREAN OCCUPATION

By the middle of July 1950, both my father and I were home, and my parents decided to evacuate our house in the center of the city to a rented house in Sajik-dong, a north end neighborhood, high on a hill, near our grandparents' smaller house. My grandfather passed away in 1947. He was troubled by the redistribution of more than a half of his landed estate in the South Ch'ungch'ong province. With Grandpa gone, Grandma and the oldest uncle decided that they did not need the oversized house, and the multi-generational family split up. Grandma and the oldest uncle and three sons relocated to a much smaller house, while the other married sons got houses of their own. Most of the household staff was released from their jobs. Our transient house was small. We were crowded into smaller spaces and had to share our rooms. But it was the wartime, and we were close to the grandma's new house. I consoled myself thinking that it could be much worse.

I was always hungry. Life in general was miserable. For the first time in my life, I thought about life and death and questioned if it was worth living. Grownups, among whom I included myself, lived with one meal a day, and men in the house lived in fear of being kidnapped into the military to the North. My father dyed his hair gray and let his beards grow, dressed in traditional Korean men's outfit, normally exclusively worn by older or retired men, and put on hollow wire-rim glasses. He looked at least 10 years older. And we hid his last remaining errand boy under the *maru*. He stayed crouched in a mud-hole, ate the food brought to him and slept on a straw mat. Most of the time, I, dressed in a little girl's outfit, stayed close to the main gate of house to watch over whether the In-min Gun would raid our house in search of young men to be recruited into their ranks. If I saw them few doors away, I would run into to inform my parents, and they would hide the errand boy in the attic, or in one remaining outhouse in the farthest corner of the backyard, covered with overgrown vines.

After I was rescued from the Youth Volunteer Corps, I did not go to school and neither did any of my younger siblings. Normally, July was the month of summer vacation in Korea and school resumed in late August. North Korean authorities, however, ran programs and propaganda all summer, and they harassed parents to send children to school, especially when the month of August rolled around. My parents would not let any of us go near any school, especially after my experience of being abducted into the volunteer corps. Besides, as the oldest child, I had to fill roles of household staff, especially of the only errand boy in hiding. Disguised as a much younger girl, I went to downtown and neighborhood shops.

I did not know the content of the paper in the sealed envelopes, which Dad gave me to deliver. I hid them in my underwear under a full-skirted dress, but I guessed that it contained the news about foreign military assistance to South Korea. I had spied that my father was listening to a short wave radio at night under beddings. He obviously had information about the state of the war that few others had and he felt obliged to share it with his close associates, for some of whom, especially those who were dissatisfied with or persecuted under President Rhee, were toying with the idea of going over to the North. The situation in July and August was desperate and many people were giving up. Knowing about the news of outside assistance might be important to make them rethink their hasty decision of going to a place of no return. Although he had been wrongfully persecuted by the South Korean regime, my father was wise, read in English language materials, and thought it through to know that what little freedom we were allowed in the South was better than not having any at all as in the North.

My parents were taking a big risk in sending me out with "secret" papers, and I was scared to death myself, but I told myself if it was important enough for my dad to put his own daughter in harm's way, it had to be really significant and that I should be willing to help. I deliberately acted cheerful and assured my parents that I would be careful and do my best to appear like an innocent little girl doing little shopping for the family. I hopped, skipped and hummed or sang songs softly. My immediate neighborhood streets were deserted, but when I was sent downtown near my father's law office in the city hall plaza, I found the center of the city in shocking disarray; there were people, mostly older men, on the streets with blank stare and aimlessly walking around while the In-min Gun soldiers marched up and down and around the circle in locked steps. Strewn on the sides of the roads and alleys were straw-mat covered human corpses, reeking decaying odors. *I could be one of the them if I ever got caught carrying a contraband material.*

My parents told me little about what was going on with the war except to assuring us that we needed to be really patient and that in the end we would be all right. In the short-term refugee house, four older kids, all girls, slept on stuffed mats on the floor in one room and three younger ones were with parents. After my younger sisters had fallen sleep, I would get up, crawl across the small *maru* to the other side of my parents' bedroom doors, put my ears close to the door, and strained to hear to make out my parents' hushed conversations. Thanks to the thin rice paper covered sliding doors, I could hear bits of their talk although much of it had a lot of complicating details that

I could not understand. But I could make out a rough outline that South Korea would not be left to be taken over by the North, that the United States referred the North Korean invasion to the United Nations, and that 15 other U.N. member states would participate in the war against Communism. What really grabbed attention and gave me a sense of relief was that the well-known American general, whose name even I as a teenager heard of, General Douglas MacArthur, was appointed as the commander of the U.S.-led United Nations forces.

But for over two long months, we heard no good news. What rumors circulated was that the size of "the Nakdong Perimeter," the unoccupied southeastern corner of the peninsula, remained the same. Even General MacArthur's first attempt at landing at Inch'on harbor in July had failed with no new known plan of when he would make another attempt. South Korea was like a candle in the storm, which would be snuffed out any time.

Toward the end of August, we began hearing thunderous cannon shots from distance. A week into September, they sounded closer. By September 10, they reverberated and shook our house as if they were exploding in our immediate neighborhood. For the next several days, we heard incessant gunshots along with mortar blasts and saw the bright lights in the center of the city. We kids huddled around our parents. Mom held the baby sister and Dad held all six of us as tightly as he could, and we stood at the edge of the *maru* and watched the city of

Seoul burning. We did not know that our city house was also being scorched at that time.

As the cannon and gunshots stopped and the fire subsided, we heard roaring cheers of people. General MacArthur's forces had landed in Inch'on on September 15 and triumphantly marched into Seoul and liberated it from the North Korean occupation.

About a week later, low-flying American airplanes sprayed the city with papers announcing that it was safe to return to the city. We also heard the same news on the radio. But my parents told us to remain in our temporary house while they and the errand boy would go down to the city house and make sure it was safe to go home. The three of them did not return until dusk. When they did, I was stunned with their appearances. Even in the dim light of early night, I could tell that all three of them were covered with soot. Mom plumped down on the edge of the *maru* and began crying.

"What are we going to do? Where are we going to live with all these kids?"

"We will make it somehow. We will have to find a new house." Dad tried to console her and he turned to us surrounding Mom and said,

"Listen, kids, carefully. Our city house burned down – almost to the ground. Don't ask us to take you there. There's nothing to be salvaged." I felt a thud in my heart. *Our house gone? All our stuff, books, notebooks, dolls and toys for the younger ones, they are all gone.* It was hard to believe, the big house and all its content. I never saw the house again for my parents did not take us and did not allow me to go to our old house until after it was completely razed to an empty lot.

"Really, is that true?" We kids asked almost in unison.

"That's right. We have to stay here until we find a suitable house, but I promise you I will do it fast so that you all can go to schools where you can attend one permanently without having to transfer repeatedly." Dad told us with unfaltering voice to give Mom and us kids sense of security. As he was talking about school, he briefly turned to me and nodded at me. I knew why. He knew that I was despondent about having no school to attend. Even in that chaos, he remembered that I had been ousted from one school and had not yet been admitted to another. He understood that school was very important to me.

I quietly thanked my father not just for his ability to rise to crisis situations but also for being sensitive to his children's individual situations.

By early October, we moved to a house on Ch'ong-un Dong, not as big and stately as our old house, but a good-sized traditional Korean house on a quiet street in the northern end of the city near the foot of the Puk'ak-san, the north peak mountain. This was the last house I lived in until I left Korea for the United States.

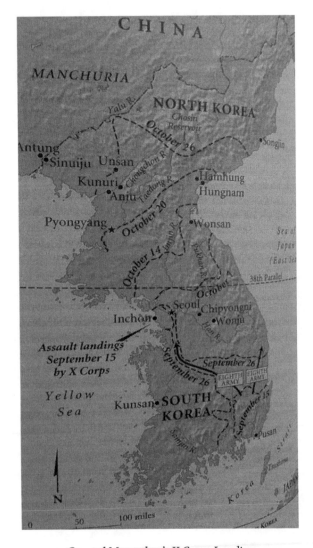

General Macarthur's X Corps Landing

15 September 1950

David Halberstam, The Coldest Winter, p. 344

CHAPTER 16:

ONE-FOUR (1.4) RETREAT

Within two weeks of General MacArthur's successful Inch'on landing, the whole of South Korea was rocked with jubilation. Even with the massive loss of lives and property, people were glad to have some semblance of normalcy. But they were about to witness an unexpected lucky turn of events. The Communists were entirely driven out of South Korea, and the U.N. forces were scoring dizzying victories. While relishing the good news, they hoped and prayed that it would last.

Our family was getting used to the new house on Ch'ong-un Dong and my younger siblings started schools in the new neighborhood. The house became quiet and more orderly allowing more time for me to study for myself. I could go out on errands for my mom in my normal clothes without the fear of being stopped, frisked, or even shot. My father reopened his law office at the city hall plaza after a massive clean up and some redecoration.

My staying home was a blessing in disguise. I had peaceful time to spend with Mom and with Grandmother when she started visiting again regularly. It was my grandmother who told me that all the terrible things that had happened, the war, near extinction, and incredible revival, occurred exactly as mentioned in *Chung Kam-rok*, a widely circulated book of prophesy since the end of the Choson dynasty. According to the volume, two foreigners, a super-human general and a sincere good civilian leader, would rescue us from red devils. General MacArthur was the military genius and adulated as demi-God, and President Truman was revered as *jin-in*, the true man, as signified in the translation of his last name.

With the phenomenal triumphs of the U.N. forces in repelling the Communist forces from South Korea, people openly talked about unifying Korea, and, as I later learned, even American public also considered a larger victory possible. Not to seize this God-given opportunity was absurd, and stopping short of accomplishing this goal was being an appeaser. Those from the North, who risked their lives to cross the border, clamored for the U.S.-led U.N. forces to march beyond the 38th parallel when they reached it by the beginning of October. Normally divisive Koreans were all united on this issue of seizing the fortuitous time and unify the country.

One late evening, I saw my father having a late night snack of dried squid with *soju*, favorite Korean clear liquor made of potatoes. October night air was cool and their door was closed, but not completely shut. Through the thin crack of the sliding door, I could see that Mom was sitting across a low-lying round red lacquer table filling the tiny *soju* cups. It had been months since I saw such a tranquil scene. Dad saw me and asked me to come in.

"I will let you stay up late because you don't have to go to school."

"Don't remind her of that. She's having a hard time as is." Mom chastised Dad.

"It's OK, Mom, I am doing a lot of reading and I sort of enjoy having time to do what I want."

"Don't get too used to it. I am seriously looking into a few schools to which you can transfer. They are saying they will have to test you to find out if you belong to your original grade and not drop you one since you are missing a whole year."

"Don't worry, Dad, I am ready for any test anyone will give me. But let's not talk about that now. I want to ask you about this rapid turn-around of the war. Can you tell me if we will have a chance to be one country again?" I wanted to divert the conversation from my school issue.

"Thank goodness, we may be one country after all. Five year's division is long enough." My father seemed genuinely pleased with the prospect. I remembered how he lamented the division when it happened.

"We will not have a border in the middle?" I asked.

"That's right. It's just an artificial line, dividing families, villages, and cities. Americans were in a hurry to stop the Russians from occupying all of the peninsula."

"So then, Appa, the country will be unified under the U.S. military?" I was curious.

"If we continue under the current condition, it's possible. I hear that General MacArthur's forces has already crossed the parallel."

"Already!" I reacted loudly.

"I heard that, too." Mom commented.

"But then, will the big Communist neighbors like the Soviets and Chinese will just watch North Korea collapse?" I pursued.

"You are asking complicating questions, my young lady. It's getting late. Run along and don't stay up too late." Dad shooed me away. It was obvious that he didn't want to go too deep into complex international situations. I was sure that he was informed of at least some of the problems, but he did not want to tell Mom and me when he was not sure of anything himself. The situation was so volatile. I deferred to Dad's advice and left to go to my room. I did not have to bug Dad to tell me what's going on, for I knew quite a bit myself. As a sixteen-year old with time on hand, I was reading all the newspapers and magazines that were available around the house.

The U.S.-led U.N. forces were raking in victory after victory through the month of October, and Koreans were delirious with the prospect of achieving the unification.

General MacArthur declared that his troops would have the Thanksgiving dinner in Pyongyang and would come home by Christmas. The complete victory of the U.N. forces and the unification of the peninsula appeared tantalizingly close.

None of us, and I learned later that even American authorities, knew at the time that at the height of U.N. victory, Chinese people's volunteer army crossed the Yalu River, the river of the border between the Korean peninsula and Manchuria. By the end of October, the first Chinese soldier was captured as POW. Even then, General MacArthur requested President Truman to approve hot pursuit of Chinese planes into Manchuria and destruction of the Yalu bridges. When Korean newspapers reported that President Truman rejected the general's proposal, Korean people were in an uproar, and their view of the American president changed overnight. He was now a villain and an enemy of Korean people while General MacArthur remained Korea's savior.

The unusually early onset of winter starting in November brought frosty news. The U.N. troops might have had Thanksgiving dinner in Pyongyang, but they were not surely going home by Christmas. In early December, the U.N. forces evacuated Pyongyang, and soon thereafter began the infamous two-week long evacuation of the X Corps, which continued until the Christmas day. Also by the middle of December, the U.N. command forces retreated below the 38th parallel. We were back to where we started three months earlier.

"This time, we are not staying in Seoul. We are going south." Dad told us one cold December afternoon.

"Bongwan, I want you to take five of your younger sisters and brothers and follow Captain Cho to take refugee in the south. The baby will stay with Mom and me."

"Me, me alone?" I shouted because I was so shocked.

"Calm down, let me finish." Dad told me sternly.

Father told us that Mom and he had to stay behind with the year-old baby sister to take care of a few important financial matters, including the issues related to the burned down house, which was about to be settled and they simply could not leave it unresolved. The future of our family depended on whether or not he completed the pending work. It would take only a few days, he said. Besides, we were not going to be completely alone. Captain Cho was accompanying us. He was a distant cousin with the same generational name and was an officer in the ROK army. He was recently married and was being transferred to Taegu, a city in north Kyongsang province. The city of Taegu was within the Pusan, or Nakdong, perimeter during the first phase of the war and would likely to be safe this time as well. Dad assured me that having Cousin Cho being stationed in Taegu was a lucky break because he could and promised to watch out for us.

Refugees trekking through the blizzard of January 1951
From the cover of Korean Politics (John Kie-chiang Oh, Cornel UP, 1999)

We became part of a huge migration of people from the Seoul area to the south in the depth of the coldest winter in Korean history. This is known as "One-Four Retreat," meaning January 4, when the Rhee government made a formal announcement, recommending people to evacuate Seoul. One early January day, I don't remember exactly which day, in the blizzard that brought several inches of snow, Mom and Dad put us on the top of straw sacks in a freight car of a long line of trains and saw us off. They repeatedly assured us that it would be only a few days and a week, at the most, before they could meet us in Taegu. Under my care were five of my younger sisters and brothers ranging in age from twelve to two and a half. I felt lucky that we were inside, certainly luckier than the people precariously perched on the snowy roof of the train. Captain Cho was with us in the same car, but he was so enamored with his bride that he hardly paid any attention to us. He stayed in the farthest corner from us.

It took us two weeks to reach Taegu, the distance of no more than five hours by train normally at the time. The train moved slowly, stopped often, and then it would slide backward a little before moving forward again. We learned later that the train machinist was a Communist sympathizer and was trying to sabotage the operation. He was waiting for the North Korean troops to return and capture the refugees. The car was so crowded that we had no room to lie down. I was crouched with my legs bent underneath to allow room for my younger siblings to stretch their legs while trying to hold each of them.

My mom and dad never imagined that we would be on the road that long. They had thought it would be a ride of no longer than several hours at its worst. The frequent stops, however, were useful for me to attend to the needs of my younger siblings' toilet, eating and drinking needs. I would take a couple of them at a time, go a little way from the train behind a tree or a fence to help them relieve, all the while stamping my feet and rushing them on for fear that the train would start any moment. Buying food and drinks were easier, for I could do it through the tiny windows of the freight car. I would buy bottles of barley tea and rolls of kimbob, sea laver rice rolls, from venders lined up along the train tracks. When the little ones ate and drank, they would smile at me and would come to give me hugs. That was all I needed to forget about all my pent-up frustration, physical discomfort, and headaches. Hard as was it was for me, harder still was watching my little brothers and sisters suffering through such unbelievable hardships at such young ages.

When we arrived at the Taegu train station, I thought I saw two hazy figures, who resembled our parents. At first, I thought I was in a dream. I shook my head to make sure I saw them right. As I was trying to figure out who they were, the younger ones obviously had no doubt. They released their hands from mine and ran to them calling, "Mom and Dad," waking me from bewilderment.

My parents had arrived at the southern city, four days after we had left. They were able to take care of business in less time than they anticipated and got a ride in an automobile, with a driver, of one of Dad's highly placed friends. They were in Taegu ten days earlier than we did. They tried but could not track down where we were and had no idea when the train would get in, and they came to the station every day to make sure they would not miss our arrival. During that time, they rented a sizable house and made necessary arrangements to ease our disloca-tion. After two and a half months in Taegu, just as we were getting used to living there, we moved again – to Pusan because, Pusan, not Taegu, was chosen to be the temporary capital of South Korea. Dad hurried our relo-cation to Pusan to be on time for the beginning of the new school year. Businesses and schools were construct-ing temporary clapboard structures to accommodate flood of refugees.

CHAPTER 17:

A REFUGEE LIFE

Pusan, located at the southeastern tip of the Korean peninsula, is now the second largest city in South Korea and is becoming its cultural capital with international film festivals and sports events. But before the flood of refugees in early 1951, it was known primarily as a beach resort town. In January 1951, it suddenly became the place to be. When we arrived there in early March of that year, I found that it was sheer madness, crowded, noisy and expensive. Anybody who was anybody in South Korea and anybody who could afford to move family from Seoul were there. Most refugees from Seoul had come directly to Pusan in January without a stopover at another city as we did. By the time we moved, there was hardly any housing left. Original Pusan people were extorting money from Seoul refugees. Even at an abominably high price, my parents could not find anything big enough to house our big family. Only place available immediately was a two-room apartment with no separate spaces for kitchen or bath, and there were ten of us including a young babysitter. Initially, three younger children, two sons and the infant, used one room with Mom and Dad and the rest of us, five daughters and the babysitter, stayed in the second larger room with a stove and a sink in one corner and the bathroom in the other. One good thing about being in Pusan was that most of Dad's clients were also there and he could continue his work.

The baby cried day and night. The poor little thing obviously sensed something was terribly wrong and cried non-stop. None of us could do anything to end her crying. To allow Father to get some sleep to go to work in the morning, she was brought to our room. But the room divide between the two rooms was paper-thin sliding doors and it helped little to muffle the baby's crying. As a last resort, Mom, the babysitter and I took turns to carry her on our backs and rock her to sleep, some times almost all through the night. In less than two weeks, the babysitter ran away. Who could blame her? She couldn't sleep at night and living condition was horrible. Even I felt like doing what she did sometimes. Some nights, I would be up until dawn with my baby sister on my back. I was exhausted and hungry and the apartment was cramped and cluttered. I was in despair. The new school year was approaching and I was not yet admitted to any school. My future looked bleak indeed.

Then, one late afternoon, my father walked in whistling a tune and motioned Mom and me to follow him. Mom and I exchanged looks and went in after him. I had my infant sister on my back, and Father called the second old sister, Bongsoon, to take the baby for a while.

As Father sat down, he told Mom and me that he had some good news.

"What good news?" Mom and I asked in unison.

"Is it about my school?" I queried Dad.

"Yes, one of two good tidings is about your school, Bongwan." I moved closer to Dad gulping down my saliva.

"I have arranged for you to be tested at Ewha Girls' High School, the school I wanted you to go in the first place."

"Ewha, that's wonderful, Dad! We couldn't do better than that."

"When do we go?"

"The day after tomorrow."

"I will be ready. Thank you, Father." I said bowing to him deeply. Mom ruffled my hair and smiled.

"What's the second good news?" Mom asked Dad.

"I am going to be a legal counsel of the Korean Tungsten Co., which is going to be established soon, no later than by the end of the year. We will be able to afford a bigger, more permanent place than we have now." The company was formally founded in 1952 and later became one of the Chaebol, conglomerate, companies, which amassed huge fortune.

"My goodness, thank you, *ch'on-ji shin-myong*, gods of heaven and earth. We are going to be all right now." Mom gathered her hands to thank the gods and said excitedly.

"You have been most patient and I appreciate that." Dad approached Mom and held her both hands. Mom lowered her head and wiped tears, tears of relief. My mom cried a lot and so do I.

Two days later, my father took me to the temporary campus of Ewha Girls' High School on Yong-do Island across the drawbridge over the Pusan Channel. It was situated at the foot of a mountain and composed of several rows of classrooms built with plywood siding and corrugated tin roof. The island was the temporary home of other elite schools from Seoul. The Kyunggi Girls' High School, my former school, was also located nearby.

Our first stop was the office of Mr. Shin Bong-jo, the principal of the school, who had been my father's teacher at Paejae boys' school.

"Welcome, please sit down. I am glad you are *finally* here." Mr. Shin said to us, emphasizing "finally."

I looked at Dad. We did not exchange words, but we knew that we were both questioning, *what does he mean by "finally?"* Dad lightly shook his head indicating to me not to worry about it.

"Mr. Cho, you should have let her come to Ewha to begin with. There was no need to have her put through this trauma. We had several girls in the similar situation but we did not expel them. It was not their fault. They were forced into the Volunteer Youth Corps, and for such a short time." Dad and I just nodded.

"Oh, well, anyway I am glad you are here," Mr. Shin continued, "Mr. Choi, vice principal for academic programs, will test her to determine what grade she is qualified to belong. I will lead you to his office but we will have to leave her alone with him and a few other teachers. You and I can come back to my office, have some tea and catch up with old times."

Principal Shin and Dad left me with Mr. Choi in a small cramped space with piles of papers and books on the desk. He sat me down on a chair across from him. He had cleared the center of his big old desk, and on both sides of the emptied center were piles of papers. After he interviewed me asking my name, address, and my father's name, occupation and facts about Mother, he excused himself and brought in three younger teachers including a young woman. Mr. Choi handed them the testing stuff and gave them instructions. I followed the three teachers outside and walked into another hut, which appeared to be a library with a few desks and chairs in the middle and bookcases around the walls. We walked over to its opposite end with a long table and chairs. The three teachers sat on one side and I was asked to sit opposite to them. I was anxious but tried to be calm by sitting upright and looking at the teachers straight ahead, not in the eye, for doing so would have been considered impolite and rude. But once the questioning began I found myself relaxed. They not only tested my knowledge of my grade's material but also tested my intelligence, which I later learned was an I.Q. test, a new test in Korea at the time, a recent import from America. Time went fast because I did not stall and was able to answer questions, oral and written, without much trouble. I heard later that I was grilled for nearly three hours.

Principal Shin and my father met me when I came out of the library shack. Mr. Shin said we needed to wait for the results at his office. I hardly had a chance to have a gulp of water when Mr. Choi came in. *Wow, so soon. That was fast.* I thought. *I hope they took time and were careful in grading my exams.* He stretched his hand to my father and said,

"Mr. Cho, congratulations. You have a smart young lady in your family. She tested high on both the regular and the I.Q. tests. She could easily skip a grade."

"On, no, I don't want her to skip a grade. As you know she didn't go to school the whole of last year and I want her to spend at least two more years before going to college."

"That's no problem. Whatever you wish, Mr. Cho." Masseurs Shin and Choi replied almost in unison.

I don't remember how the rest of the day went and how Dad and I got home. I was so happy. All I remember now is that I felt as if a high wall was removed from in front of me, making me feel as if a wide road had opened up. When Dad and I returned to our tiny apartment, Mom had prepared a big table with many delicious dishes that we had not had in months. The table filled the room almost entirely, and we had to squeeze through to sit down. I don't know how she knew about my test results, where she got all that good stuff and when she had time to prepare that much – all by herself without any help. We had the first joyful family dinner in Pusan. Even the baby stopped crying that night and less fussy from that day on.

Two weeks later, we moved to a house, a freestanding structure with many rooms, near the Yong-do Bridge. I didn't realize at the time but it is obvious that my parents timed the relocation to be in time for the new academic year and selected the house to be near the island where schools were congregated. We lived in the house for two and a half years, and I started my second year of high school on the refugee campus of Ewha Girls' High School and entered the college while living there.

I found Ewha different from Kyunggi to the degree to make me wonder how two girls' high schools in the same city of a small country like Korea could be so different. The Ewha's teachers paid considerable attention to individual students and the school's organization was less structured allowing each student considerable freedom. This led Ewha to have somewhat less favorable reputation among high-society Korean parents that it permitted liberty to adolescent women. Having attended three middle school years at Kyunggi, I too needed a little adjustment at first, but I came to like the atmosphere, especially when they permitted us to choose between science and non-science classes. I selected the humanities and social sciences class.

Two years later on a cool day in late March, we gathered on the bumpy ground with rickety chairs for the graduation ceremony. The graduates were seated in the front section and the parents behind us. After speeches and choirs, my turn came to give the valedictory address. As I went up the wobbly platform, the principal rose unexpectedly and said,

"Graduates, parents, and ladies and gentlemen, I am truly proud to present this student to you as this year's valedictorian. Do you know who she is? She is the daughter of one of my former, most successful students, whom I taught when I was a high school teacher. Would the parents of Cho Bong-wan, please rise." He put his right hand out to where my parents were seated and gestured them to get up. My parents looked around and hesitantly stood up. The crowd broke into loud cheers and applause.

"There's more than that. Do you know where she will go to college? The Law College of Seoul National University, tenth in a class of 200! Imagine that, a woman in a men's university! She honored Ewha and all of us." The audience gave a standing ovation.

I looked at my parents. Father was shaking his clasped hands in my direction. His lips were moving. I was sure he was telling me he was proud of me. My mother was dabbing her eyes with her handkerchief.

My war ended on that March day in 1953 although the Korean War would go on another four months.

CHAPTER 18:
A STEALTHY PREPARATION

My parents were delighted that I was admitted to my father's *alma mater*, Seoul National University, the aspirational school for most college-bound young people in Korea, and one that was difficult to be admitted to, even for young men. It was a big deal that a woman got in. The ratio between men and women were 20 to 1 in 1953. I was looking forward to studying with the brightest of the lots and to become a learned lawyer or a judge, following in my father's footsteps. My parents and I never thought about any other career for me. I was the oldest child, considered bright and hard working.

About a semester into the freshman year, I began to recognize serious problems. Korea was in chaos in the aftermath of the devastating war. There was no infrastructure anywhere, and education was no exception. There was no orderly system of instruction. Professors literally peddled their knowledge at several different colleges and universities to make their ends meet. The classes were routinely cancelled for their no-shows. When they were held, they either started late or were dismissed early. SNU was such a difficult school to enter, but little learning and teaching were going on.

I was disappointed, for I was not gaining enough knowledge. My hope of getting solid liberal arts foundation to become a wise judge or lawyer was not being realized. I tried to do a lot of reading on my own but was frustrated. Many ambitious young male classmates from elite high schools simply did not attend classes. Instead, they took turns to come to campus with a handful of seals, to stamp on the attendance book. With the encouragement of their parents, they packed up to spend extended periods of time at Buddhist temples in the mountains to concentrate on studies to pass *Koshi*, the civil service examination. Passing the state examination was considered more important than the college education. It was considered the ultimate to be admitted to the bar and to be appointed to judgeships or to practice law. One of my classmates who did just that later became a judge in the Korean Supreme Court and a presidential candidate.

But, it was unthinkable for a young woman, to be away from home at a far away place for a prolonged period. My parents would never send me to an isolated Buddhist temple for any length of time. I either continue being a dilettante college kid and get a diploma or do something drastic. I agonized over what to do for a long time. Where could I go to receive a substantive under-graduate education? As a student at the Seoul National University, the best and most coveted university in the country, there was no place to go within Korea but to step down. After a while, I decided that I had to go out-side the country to study, England, France or America. But I knew no body in any of these countries.

I decided to do some research. Starting in the sec-ond semester of the freshman year, I stopped by the office of the United States Information Agency (USIA), an annex of the U.S. embassy in Korea. I was amazed with the volume of materials on America, huge color-ful glossy magazines, *Life*, weekly news magazines of *Time* and *Newsweek*, and many other dazzling publica-tions. I passed these display isles fighting the temptation to thumb through them and followed a staff person to a quiet corner with rows of catalogues of all the colleges and universities in the United States. I was surprised again. There were so many. I didn't know where to start. After talking to a kind staff, I learned about Ivy League universities for men and Seven Sisters' colleges for women. Perhaps, young, brash and audacious, I thought I could not go to any school with less stature and pres-tige than Seoul National University. I had to go to a best college in America, hopefully one of the Seven Sisters' colleges.

My parents had absolutely no idea what I was doing. I went behind my parents' back, for the first time in my life. The goody, goody daughter was hiding things from parents, how awful! When I thought about my parents, I would lose courage, but I had to do this. My future depended on what I decided at that juncture in my life. I had no idea where this daredevil attitude came to me. I had been such a docile obedient daughter until that time. One thing was for sure. I had to prepare myself, for I knew that I had a very slim chance of getting their consent unless I presented them a *fait accompli*. I had to present to them something they could not object if they were being reasonable, which they were most of the time.

I applied to three colleges, Radcliffe, Barnard, and Vassar.

Realizing that a simple query letter from a war-torn underdeveloped, dirty and poor Korea would get nowhere, I made my query packet that no admissions personnel could simply discard. In the first mailing, I enclosed all the information an admission's committee would want to know about me: an autobiographical essay, a passport size, but a smiling photo, high school and college transcripts, and recommendations. And I waited. A couple of months after I mailed the application packets, I came home early every day from school and picked up the mail myself. On the days I couldn't come home early enough, I bribed a maid to bring my mail to my room.

In early summer of 1955, I began receiving fat envelopes in quick succession. I couldn't believe it, but it was true, that I was admitted to all three with offers for scholarships! From the beginning I was less interested in Vassar, for it was in the countryside, and I had been a city girl all my life. I compared the offers from Radcliffe and Barnard Colleges. The latter offered a more generous scholarship, and it was in New York City. The thought of studying in New York was simply beyond my imagination. My heart pounded. I felt like shouting to the world, but I could tell no one. I had no older siblings and no friends with whom I could share this exciting news. Cousin Soon had moved on and was no longer living at my house. I also had to play cool with my parents. One misstep could undo all my effort of the past year.

I sat on the good news from the U.S. for several restless days and sleepless nights to look for a propitious moment to break the news to my parents. But the deadlines were approaching. One late summer evening in 1955, my Dad returned home later than usual in a particularly good mood. I could tell he had a few drinks. On those nights, he would usually gather his children and tell us stories of his childhood in the country, our ancestors, and importance of education regardless of one's gender. I loved these nights. After my younger siblings had gone to bed, I would fill the wine cups for my dad and he would continue to talk about his ideals, hopes for world peace and for his children. I would listen to him with apt attention deep into the night. Many a night, it would be just Dad and me.

That night, I caught onto the part of his talk about education and seized the opportunity.

"Speaking of education, do you know, *Appa*, that there is hardly any learning going on at the university?" He was surprised.

"How can it be? You are at the best school with the brightest kids."

"That's just it, *Appa*. Professors are peddling their knowledge at too many colleges and universities because they get paid so little. I would like to get more solid college education, which is supposed to be the basis of a person's make-up for his/her entire life."

"That's a shame! What can you do about it?"

"So, I was thinking . . ."

"What were you thinking?"

"Would you promise you wouldn't get mad at me?"

"Mad at you? Why? I don't get upset with you too often, do I?"

I nodded but said nothing for a while.

My mother, who had been listening quietly, became impatient and persuaded me to tell them what I had in mind. After a while, I just blurted it out.

"I got into three top women's colleges in the U.S."

"What? How?"

My parents appeared dumbfounded. They told me to get the packets. I rushed out and got the thick envelopes from the American schools. Dad looked at them. He was one of few among his peers who could read English.

"You did all this by yourself? Who helped you?"

"Nobody."

"Really? How?"

I told them. My parents looked at each other their mouths halfway open and then turned to me. I had my head bowed. After what seemed like an eternity, I stole a look at my Dad. Even as he was surprised and shocked, I detected a slight, very slight, smile on his face. I breathed a quiet sigh of relief.

"Let me think about this a couple of days. I will first have to read the papers very carefully, and then, your mom and I will have to talk this through and will let you know." I was sure I heard my father, but it seemed like it was coming from a far away place. For a fleeting moment, I was already worried about how I was going to leave home. My father's voice brought me back to reality.

"Don't worry about this tonight. It's very late. Go get some sleep."

I stood up, stepped back a few steps. As I was closing the sliding door of their room, I made a deep bow and said,

"Thank you, *Appa, Umma*, for being reasonable. I knew you would be. Please don't take too long though. I have deadlines coming up soon, very soon." I was so glad they did not say outright "no."

CHAPTER 19:

BUTTERFINGER

Early February of 1956, I packed two suitcases with what I thought I would need in a new country and prepared to board one of the first few Pan Am trans-Pacific flights to the United States. The Kimp'o Airport, the only airport at the time in South Korea, consisted of leftover make-shift buildings from the American military. The only paved grounds were a few runways. Several military planes were parked on the tarmac, but only one Pan-Am airplane was waiting for passengers. It had snowed a few days earlier, then rained, and snow had melted. The flurries were coming down again but not heavy yet. The grounds were so soggy that they had laid down plywood sheets for departing passengers and those that had come to see them off. Even so, the mud oozed up between the cracks and dirtied our shoes.

I was wearing a new forest green overcoat with a matching hat, which were specially made by a tailor shop at Myong-dong, a fashionable shopping district. I wore a new camel-colored cashmere scarf and a new pair of shoes with an inch and a half stacked heel. Mom said I needed a little boost in height because I was going to a country of tall people. I also had a new tan-colored leather shoulder bag, which was bigger than the handbags I normally carried. Even so, it was so full of stuff that I could hardly close it. I was wearing everything new, some of which I had wanted for a long time. I was sorry that many of my friends at the university would not get to see me with all the fancy stuff I had on.

The party at the airport to see me off was huge: my parents, all six of my younger siblings, and uncles, aunts, and cousins. Even my grandmother came to see me off. There were also many of my college and high school classmates. Almost all of twenty female students in my Law College class of 200 came out, and about a dozen guys also showed up. My male friends stayed somewhat apart from my family and sheepishly waved or used other gestures to let me know that they were there. But my women pals were all over me and admired my new coat, shoes and handbag, asking where I got them and how much they cost. My mom knew some of them and answered their queries, for I was busy greeting people.

I did not realize that I mattered that much to all of them. I thought, *if they liked me so much why didn't they let me know before?* I was close to some of them, of course, but others—especially the guys—I had no idea that they knew I even existed. I thought it was almost

like people showing appreciation and heaped compli-
ments after death. I assumed that perhaps it was not I,
per se, but the novelty of a young woman going away
so far to study. In those days, once one left home to go
abroad, the letters were the only means of communica-
tion and they usually took a month to get responses. It
was almost like disappearing into a never-never land,
perhaps never to return. So, I was about to embark on a
journey into an unknown world.

I was grateful so many people had braved the bad
weather to see me off. At first, I was busy going around
shaking hands, hugging and chatting. And then, it
dawned on me that it was me to whom people were saying goodbye. Suddenly, I could not greet them properly
or say goodbye, even to my younger siblings, for I was
all choked up. My mom turned her back to me after a
quick, short hug. She obviously did not want to show
me her tears. She was the one, who had always told me
about the legend of my paternal grandmother, who supposedly did not shed a drop of tears when she was sending my dad off to Seoul to study when he was only thirteen years old. Mother's mantra to us daughters was that
even women had to be educated and strong to survive
in the tough new world. Now she was sending me off to
study and she did not want to go back on her own words.

At the last minute, just before entering the final gate,
my dad walked over close to me and slipped something into my coat pocket. I stuck my hand in and felt a
couple of stick-like things. I took them out. They were

Butterfinger bars. Surprised, I looked up at him with my mouth open.

"I know. Just in case you need some quick energy," Dad said, anticipating my question.

"Oh, *Appa*, these are my favorites, but how did you know?"

"I know a few things about you."

"Thank you, *Appa*." I gave him a hug and a quick peck on his cheek. When I quickly looked up, his eyes were red and moist.

"Get going." Dad directed me. "As a saying goes, 'those who have to go, must not delay.'"

He quickly turned around, held my youngest sister's hand and led the rest of my well-wishers away. But Mom remained behind and gently pushed me to the gate. The entrance doors shut behind me with a big clang. I resented that the doors closed so quickly and loudly. It seemed as if the loud sound was permanently severing me from my family and friends. I looked back and looked through the dirty glass panels of the top half of the doors. I could see Mom and Grandma waiving hands wiping their eyes with handkerchiefs. I moved my heavy feet around headed toward the door leading to the waiting plane outside, fingering the Butterfinger wrappings in my pocket.

~~~~~~~~~~

I was not the only young Korean pursuing the ideal of higher education in the United States following the end of the Korean War. By 1965, nearly three thousand Korean students would come to America to study. Many of them, especially the men, traveled for weeks on freighters. I journeyed on one of the first flights across the Pacific on the Pan American World Airways. Passenger air travel was still in its infancy, particularly the trans-Pacific route, and at that time it took Pan Am thirty-three hours to cover the distance from Tokyo to San Francisco. My travel time to New York was supposed to be two days, but was far longer, for we made a number of stops, both planned and unplanned. There was a layover in Tokyo to pick-up passengers, a stop at Wake Island to refuel and repair an engine, a change of planes at San Francisco, and a night spent waiting out a storm in Kansas City, Missouri. I arrived more than two days late.

When I landed at New York's Idlewild airport, it was 4:30 on the morning of February 14, 1956. By the time a taxi driver dropped me off an hour later in front of the Brooks Hall of Barnard College, I was sad, tired, and disheveled. I rang the doorbell in the columned stone porch of the dorm building, expecting to wait a while because of the early morning hours. To my surprise, a middle-aged woman in a robe of a dusty-rose shade immediately answered the door. She had to have been awake waiting for me. I thought a sincere apology. *Thank you and I am so sorry to have you wait so long.* Almost instantly she threw her arms around me in an enveloping hug.

"You must be Bongwan," she said. "I was sick to death worrying about you."

It was Ms. Harriet Benson, my first housemother at Barnard College. I buried my head in her bosom and cried shamelessly. As I was led into a high ceiling parlor, carpeted with exquisite Oriental rugs, through the heavy double doors of stained glass, I felt safe and warm as if I had reached my "home away from home."

As I was led up the circular stairs with one hand on the iron railing and the other in the coat pocket, I felt the Butterfinger bars. They got all crushed and melted. Chocolate oozed out on to my hand. I licked it. I sent silent messages to my parents. *Thanks, Dad, for the candy and every thing you've done for me, and Mom, for getting me ready for this journey. I think I am going to be all right now.*

EPILOGUE

I spent three and a half years at Barnard, majoring in history. During my junior year, I met my future husband, John Kie-chiang Oh, a Columbia graduate student in international studies who was also serving as the press attaché at the Korean Mission to the U.N. He was a native of Korea, a captain in the Korean War, and a bilingual reporter at the Panmunjom Armistice conference that stopped the war. Highly regarded by other Korean students in New York, he was a handsome, smart young diplomat who was continuing with his post-baccalaureate education. Our friends encouraged the match—each of us was told the other was "a good catch."

Captain Kie-chiang Oh at Panmunjom, Korea, Spring 1953

On 5 September 1959, we got married in Washington, D.C. My husband had resigned from his entry-level diplomat's job and left the Big Apple to dedicate full-time to his studies. Both of us enrolled in Georgetown University graduate school, my husband for his doctorate in international relations, and I for the master's degree in history.

Three children, two daughters and a son, Jane Junghwa, Marie Jaehwa, and James Jaeyong, came in quick succession. Throughout childbearing, rearing and home making, I continued my graduate work with encouragement from my husband. In 1974, when my oldest child, Jane, was fourteen years old, I finally received a doctorate in East Asian civilization from the Center for Far Eastern Studies of the University of Chicago. Since then until retirement in 2006, I had held university-level teaching and administrative positions at five universities and colleges.

Our children are now in their early 50s, thriving at the prime of their lives: Jane, as a physician, and Marie and Jimmy, as attorneys. They have all been married over twenty years and gifted my husband and me with eight grandchildren, two granddaughters and six grandsons. My husband of over fifty years passed away in the spring of 2010.

Our 50ʰ wedding anniversary party at our son's house
Wilmette, Illinois, on August 30, 2009

In the summer of 2012, I brought my entire family of fifteen to Korea. I wanted to fulfill my late husband's dream of traveling to Korea, all together as a family, to introduce our native land to our American-born children, their spouses, and grandchildren. His time ran out while waiting for the youngest grandson to be old enough to travel overseas. I also wanted to celebrate three oldest grandsons' high school graduations. My grandchildren called it a "once-in-a lifetime trip." I did not have to tell them. They knew—it was Grandpa's legacy.

The Hubers, Murneys, and Ohs on the grounds of the Blue House, The Korean Presidential Palace, on August 3, 2012

GLOSSARY

Ahboji . . . . Father

Anbang. . . . . . . Interior room, usually reserved for
matriarch of the family

Anch'ae . . . . . . Inner living quarter of a traditional
Korean house

Appa . . . . Dad, papa

Assi . . . . Ma'am

Binyo. Hairpin

Bolyo. . . . . .A thick, embroidered silk mat,
usually placed in the center end
of a room, reserved for the oldest
person in presence

Byongp'ung . . . . Paneled screen

Chaebol . . . . . Financial and business conglomerate
in South Korea

Ch'ima . . . . Skirt

Chojori . . . . A jacket of traditional attire

Ch'on-ji shin-myong. . . . . Gods of heaven and earth,
indigenous nature worship gods
in Korea

Chung Kam-rok . . . . . . A widely circulated book of
prophesy since the end of the
Choson dynasty

Darak. . . . . Attic

Duitch'ae. . . . . . . Rear, servant quarter also known as
Sarangch'ae

Halmoni . . . . Grandmother

Han'gul . . . . Korean alphabet

Hyon-mo yang-ch'o . . . . Wise mother and good wife

Jjajangmyon . . . . . . Noodles with black-bean sauce,
originally from China but a favorite
dish in Korea

Jesa. . . . . Ancestral worship ceremony,
performed on the anniversaries of death

Kimbob . . . . Sea laver rice rolls, commonly
known in America as *nori maki*,
Japanese translation

Koshi. . . . . The civil service examination,
an entry into government service

Kwang . . . . Storage shed

Maru . . . . Center, all purpose hall of
a traditional house

Noona . . . . .Older sister used by younger male
sibling

Obi . . . . Japanese bridal sash

Ondol. . . . . Floor heated through a flue from
outside, traditional heating since
the seventh century in Korea

Paji . . . . Pants of traditional men's attire

Soju . . . . .A favorite Korean clear liquor made
of potatoes

Sarangch'ae . . . . Outer section of a traditional house,
reserved for patriarch of the family,
also known as Duitch'ae

Sarang . . . . Love (a noun and verb)

Umma . . . . Mommy

Unni . . . . .Older sister

Yi Dynasty (1392-1910) . . . . . The last royal dynasty
of Korea